The crags of North Carolina's Grandfather Mountain overlook Linville Gorge.

Blue Ridge Range
The Gentle Mountains

By Ron Fisher

Photographed by
Richard Alexander Cooke III

Prepared by the Book Division
National Geographic Society, Washington, D.C.

BLUE RIDGE RANGE
The Gentle Mountains

By Ron Fisher
Photographed by
    Richard Alexander Cooke III

Published by
The National Geographic Society
Reg Murphy, *President and*
    Chief Executive Officer
Gilbert M. Grosvenor,
    Chairman of the Board

Nina D. Hoffman, *Senior Vice President*

Prepared by The Book Division
William R. Gray,
    Vice President and Director
Charles Kogod,
    Assistant Director
Barbara A. Payne, *Editorial Director*
    and Managing Editor

Staff for this book
Margaret Sedeen, *Managing Editor*

Thomas B. Powell III,
    Illustrations Editor
Suez B. Kehl, *Art Director*
Susan C. Eckert, Timothy H. Ewing,
    Melanie Patt-Corner, *Researchers*
Richard M. Crum, Margaret Sedeen,
    Jennifer C. Urquhart,
    Picture Legend Writers
Susan M. Carlson, *Map Art and*
    Research
Susan C. Eckert, *Map Research*
Sandra F. Lotterman, *Editorial Assistant*

Karen Dufort Sligh,
Illustrations Assistant

Lewis R. Bassford,
Production Project Manager

Heather Guwang, H. Robert Morrison,
Richard S. Wain, *Production*

Karen F. Edwards, Elizabeth G.
Jevons, Artemis S. Lampathakis,
Teresita Cóquia Sison,

Marilyn J. Williams, *Staff Assistants*

*Manufacturing and
Quality Management*
George V. White, *Director*
    John T. Dunn, *Associate Director*
    Vincent P. Ryan, *Manager*
    and R. Gary Colbert

Dianne L. Hardy, *Indexer*

Copyright © 1992, 1998
National Geographic Society.

*The sheer cliffs of Whiteside Mountain
rise in North Carolina's Nantahala
National Forest.*

*PRECEDING PAGES: A mountain
meadow in northern Georgia finds new
life on an artist's canvas.*

Contents

*On the edge of South Carolina's Sumter National Forest,
the exuberant cascade of Long Creek Falls tumbles toward its rendezvous
with a wild white-water stretch of the Chattooga River.*

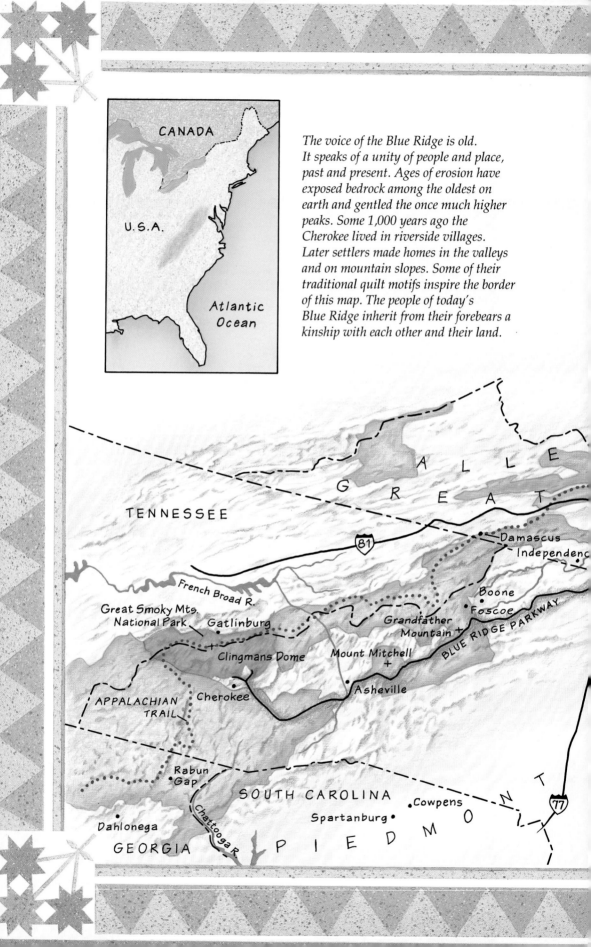

The voice of the Blue Ridge is old.
It speaks of a unity of people and place,
past and present. Ages of erosion have
exposed bedrock among the oldest on
earth and gentled the once much higher
peaks. Some 1,000 years ago the
Cherokee lived in riverside villages.
Later settlers made homes in the valleys
and on mountain slopes. Some of their
traditional quilt motifs inspire the border
of this map. The people of today's
Blue Ridge inherit from their forebears a
kinship with each other and their land.

CANADA

U.S.A.

Atlantic
Ocean

GREAT VALLEY

TENNESSEE

81

Damascus
Independence

French Broad R.

Great Smoky Mts.
National Park   Gatlinburg

Boone
Foscoe

Grandfather
Mountain

BLUE RIDGE PARKWAY

Clingmans Dome

Mount Mitchell

Asheville

APPALACHIAN
TRAIL

Cherokee

Rabun
Gap

SOUTH CAROLINA

Cowpens

Chattooga R.

Spartanburg

PIEDMONT

77

Dahlonega

GEORGIA

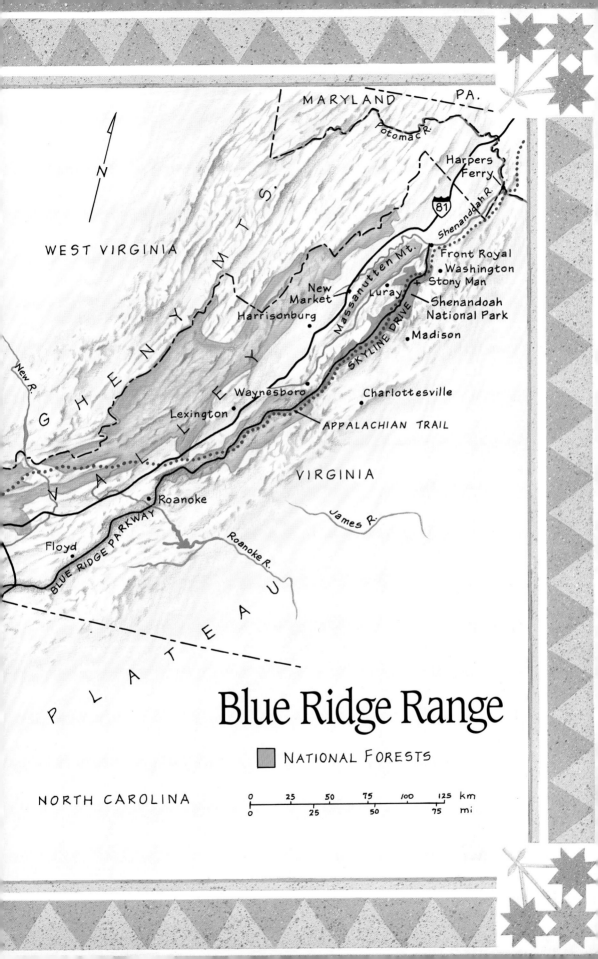

Blue Ridge Range

NATIONAL FORESTS

| 0 | 25 | 50 | 75 | 100 | 125 | km |
| 0 | | 25 | | 50 | 75 | mi |

*Cresting in an ocean of mist,
the Blue Ridge Mountains
roll out of antiquity and enfold
the lore of Indians, explorers,
and settlers from
Pennsylvania to Georgia.*

BEGINNINGS

A S OLD AS THE HILLS, we say, and it's probably the Blue Ridge Mountains we're thinking of. This battered and misty rumple in the skin of North America seems to have been always old, to have been there from our beginnings, to have fostered the aged artifacts of our eastern mountain folklore and folk life: old quilts and old storytellers, old legends and myths and folk remedies, old fiddlers and old songs, old dances, old byways, churches, skills, and crafts, old battles, old cabins.

These hills were old when only American Indians—those we know as the Cherokee—lived here a thousand years ago. The Cherokee were a large and powerful nation, in the same linguistic family as the Iroquois. They lived in square or rectangular bark-covered houses, farmed corn, beans, and squash, and hunted and fished in their mountain coves and valleys. They kept dogs as pets. They called the Blue Ridge Mountains "the blue wall." They also called them "the unending mountains," not so much for their physical dimensions as for their timeless aura. The Blue Ridge Mountains "speak of the past and its continuity with us" wrote North Carolinian William A. Bake.

The Blue Ridge Range is the easternmost ridge of the southern Appalachian Mountains. Our story covers the area between Harpers Ferry, West Virginia, and northern Georgia. Other smaller ranges, among them the Great Smokies, are a part of the Blue Ridge. The Great Valley, which consists of the Shenandoah and Tennessee Valleys, parallels the Blue Ridge to the west, and the Piedmont Plateau, the "foot of the mountains," lies to the east. In the south, the Blue Ridge settles into the central plains of Georgia, and in the north it ends just across the Potomac River in Maryland and Pennsylvania.

The empire of the Cherokee spilled beyond the boundaries of the Blue Ridge, encompassing at its zenith parts of what would become eight states. There were an estimated 20,000 to 30,000

Deft needlework fashioned this quilt, displayed by Verlene and Ernest Roark in Boone, North Carolina. The old craft of hand-stitching scraps of cloth into coverlets of exuberant design expresses a value deeply treasured in the Blue Ridge, the sharing of skills and heirlooms with family and friends.

Cherokee living when they first encountered whites. The Spanish explorer Hernando de Soto, searching for gold, marched through Georgia—and perhaps through North Carolina and Tennessee as well—not quite 50 years after the landing of Columbus. He rendered the word Cherokee as "Chalaque." He had been in Peru with Pizarro and had learned there how to deal with simple Indians: Torture them for information, and kill those who won't talk. Not surprisingly, the Indians repeatedly told him that the gold he was seeking was in the next valley over. Of all the Appalachian explorers, naturalist Donald Culross Peattie wrote, de Soto was "the worst—the cruelest, most fantastic, the briefest, and the least appreciative. Little that we can recognize as peculiarly Appalachian in its flavor comes out from his chronicles; the mountains to him were a stone in his greedy path, on which he stumbled, and cursed as only a Christian can."

The Cherokee nation produced some notable men, including Junaluska, who helped Gen. Andrew Jackson turn the tide against the Creek Indians at Horseshoe Bend, Alabama, in 1814, and Sequoyah, who, a few years later, gave his people an alphabet and the gift of reading and writing. Long fascinated with the "talking leaves" of the whites, he examined their newspapers and, after much study, assigned a symbol to each of the sounds in the Cherokee language. He needed 86 characters. Within weeks, Cherokee children and elders alike were reading and writing.

For 150 years, the high, rugged, forested Blue Ridge Mountains were a barrier beyond which settlement from the east did not venture. But by the 1750s and 1760s, pioneers were moving alongside the mountains, southward from Pennsylvania and northwestward from Charleston, South Carolina. By 1776 the Piedmont and a few valleys in the mountains were thinly populated. Many of the newcomers from Pennsylvania had originated in the province of Ulster in Ireland, where Presbyterian Scots had settled in the time of Oliver Cromwell. "In the wake of the first Scots settlers came the Germans," wrote historian Armistead C. Gordon. "As the Ulstermen thereafter were known as Scotch-Irish, the Germans were called the Valley Dutch. To neither race was the appellation, which it received and still keeps, appropriate." Settlers found the mountains, and even the valleys, practically empty, used primarily as a hunting ground and as a roadway between north and south. A well-marked trail along the crest of the Blue Ridge would become Skyline Drive; another in the valley would turn first into the Valley Pike, then into U.S. Route 11, which roughly parallels Interstate 81.

"The Tidewater discovered, but the Tidewater did not settle the Valley," wrote historian Julia Davis. In 1716 the lieutenant governor of Virginia, Sir Alexander Spotswood, who was fascinated by westward settlement and expansion, led an expedition of 50 well-provisioned men into the Blue Ridge, searching for a route to the Great Lakes. When they returned home, each man was presented with a golden horseshoe as a memento of his trip and thus became, in Virginia myth and legend, a Knight of the Golden Horseshoe.

English settlers stayed mostly in the northern end of the Shenandoah Valley, where good land spread for some 30 miles between the mountains. Capt. Ferdinand Marie Bayard of Paris visited Winchester in 1791 and spoke of "this region where, beneath skies almost always serene, the inhabitants cultivate a generous soil."

In the coves and hollows of the mountains, other settlers cleared tiny farms, usually near a spring. Log cabins, which were introduced from Sweden, sprang up, and rail fences rimmed fields. From sourwood trees, whose long, white, tassel-like blossoms provide bees with nectar, the pioneers harvested delicious honey, and from the woods, meadows, fields, and swamps around them they gathered the raw materials for the utensils, clothing, bedding, furniture, and musical instruments they made for themselves. Cash was practically unknown.

Gardens and orchards produced fruit and vegetables, and the barnyard provided chickens, milk, and bacon. The everyday fabric was linsey-woolsey, a coarse, homespun material woven of wool and linen or cotton. It and other fabrics were tinted with a variety of vegetable dyes: sumac for tan, walnut for browns and black, indigo for blue, hickory bark for green, sedge grass with alum for yellow, maple bark with copperas for purple. Baskets were woven and pots and pitchers turned on crude wheels. Corn shucks became chair bottoms or children's dolls.

During the French and Indian War, the Cherokee had sided with the colonists against the French, but by the time of the American Revolution they had identified their real enemies and fought with the British against the Americans. They paid for this error in judgment for decades to come.

In eastern Tennessee, Cherokee warriors ascended mountain rivers and killed a number of settlers. Across the mountains in South Carolina, Cherokee and Tories attacked a fort and killed more whites. Enraged colonists retaliated with 7,000 troops in a multipronged attack. They were the first American army to traverse the Blue Ridge, crossing the mountains by way of the watershed of the French Broad River at Swannanoa Gap in August 1776. They destroyed Indian towns throughout the southern mountains.

The Revolutionary War barely touched the Blue Ridge, though mountain men fought in the conflict. A couple of battles took place in or near the mountains. At Kings Mountain in South Carolina the Patriots defeated a British army of 1,125 men and killed their commander, Maj. Patrick Ferguson. And later, at Cowpens, a grassy pasture in the scrub-pine forest of South Carolina, American Continentals and backwoods militia defeated a British force commanded by "Bloody Tarleton"—Col. Banastre Tarleton. The battle was fought by small forces and lasted barely an hour but was a resounding victory for the Patriots: The British lost 110 dead, 200 wounded, 500 captured. Of the Americans, 12 were killed and 62 wounded.

Walk today across the grassy clearing at Cowpens and it's difficult to summon the passions that made the blood flow here on the morning of January 17, 1781. Visitors stroll along in hot sunshine, dodging joggers, as jets make quiet contrails high overhead. Wild yellow roses bloom alongside the paths, and in the distance the pale line of the Blue Ridge rises on the horizon.

"Near this location, General Daniel Morgan . . ." reads a signboard. Morgan exhorted his troops before the battle, calling them "my friends in arms, my dear boys." He charged them to remember Saratoga, Monmouth, Paoli, Brandywine. "This day, you must play your parts for honor and liberty's cause."

Another signboard marks the spot where Col. William Washington, second cousin to George, fought hand to hand with Tarleton, whose parting shot hit Washington's horse.

The cowpens were just that, pastures where cattle grazed. Nearby springs and lush grass and peavine made the areas popular with cattlemen, and trampling hooves kept the forest free of undergrowth: good terrain for a battle. The long whips of the cattle drovers may have given rise to the once innocent but now pejorative nickname "cracker," as in Georgia Cracker.

The population of the Blue Ridge Range during this time was small. Horace Kephart, in *Our Southern Highlanders*, wrote that during the Revolution "the mountain region itself remained almost uninhabited by whites, because the pioneers who crossed it were seeking better hunting grounds and farmsteads than the mountains afforded. It was not until the buffalo and elk and beaver had been driven out of Tennessee and Kentucky, and those rolling savannahs were being fenced and tilled, that much attention was given to the mountains proper."

Many veterans of the Revolutionary Army received land grants for their service, and German, Scotch-Irish, and English farms appeared in ever greater numbers in the Great Valley. Around the Smokies, settlers pushed their way up the valleys and streams of eastern Tennessee and western North Carolina, fostering the imagery we carry still of the mountain families: gathering ginseng, churning butter, milling and blacksmithing, carpentering and making soap, constructing stills, whittling on the porch. What we now call mountain crafts evolved from need: If a pioneer family wanted a chair or a new hinge for the door, they made it; if they broke a crock, they found some clay and made another. Ragged clothing found new life in patchwork quilts. There was a further need that the people filled, perhaps instinctively: for beauty. As form followed function, their furniture and baskets and bedding achieved a grace that delights us still. Mountain craftspeople now strive to emulate the work of their ancestors.

There grew up, early in this century, a tradition of "Yankee schoolmarms," often tough New England women who made it their mission to come to the southern Appalachians and establish schools to educate the mountain children. Hundreds were founded and a number still exist, either as craft schools, college-preparatory schools, or liberal arts colleges. Berea College, Alice Lloyd College, Berry College, Tallulah Falls School, and Rabun Gap-Nacoochee School are a few.

The pioneers became expert at finding uses for the plants they found growing around them. The ginseng industry was well established by early in the 1800s. Its name derived from the Chinese *jen shen*. It is still shipped to China and elsewhere in the Orient, where medicine subscribes to the doctrine of signatures: Any tonic brewed from a plant having the same shape as the afflicted organ is beneficial. Thus, since many ginseng roots resemble a complete human figure, the plant is considered a cure-all. It grows wild throughout the southern Blue Ridge. *(Continued on page 26)*

Restored cabin and outhouse in South Carolina preserve ways typical
of mountain folk in the 1800s. A scooped-out tree trunk furnished the
big front-porch chair. On the log-and-mud wall hangs an old bear trap.

FOLLOWING PAGES: *In early spring, a soft filigree of flowering dogwood dapples a glen on Tennessee's Little Pigeon River in the Great Smokies, haven of the largest uncut hardwood forest in North America.*

LARRY ULRICH

Thomas Jefferson's "own dear Monticello" harbors 1,000 acres of forest, orchards, vineyards, and gardens. The red of the cockscomb (below) is echoed in Jefferson's bedroom. He used the polygraph on the table to automatically copy letters as he wrote them. Jefferson's architectural plans incorporated the first dome built on an American house. Jefferson died in his bed on July 4, 1826, the 50th anniversary of the Declaration of Independence.

Encampment of Confederate reenactors stirs to life on a May morning near New Market, Virginia. In 1864 the Civil War jolted the sleepy farm town into history. Seeking control of the agriculturally rich Shenandoah Valley, a Union army (opposite) 6,000 strong occupied the town and laid down a withering fire as outnumbered Rebels counterattacked. To hold the center of his line, Southern Gen. John Breckinridge called up 257 teenage cadets from nearby Virginia Military Institute. In a daring charge the cadets captured a cannon as the Federals broke and ran. The Battle of New Market stands as the last Confederate victory in the Shenandoah Valley.

Owner of what was the largest gold mining operation east of the Mississippi, Bryan Whitfield inspects a glory hole. Miners at Dahlonega, Georgia, excavated the 250-foot stope by tunneling under a vein of gold, then boring upward. In the 16th century, Spanish explorers futilely combed the Blue Ridge in search of gold. In 1828, near Dahlonega, a deer hunter stumbled over a gold-veined rock and set off the nation's first gold rush. The scramble for wealth by outsiders uprooted most of the Cherokee and, in 1838, led to their removal on the infamous Trail of Tears. Gold fever still lingers in the Blue Ridge, but the prospectors of today are mainly amateur rock hounds who pan for gold.

Hundreds of other plants were more useful to the pioneers. In *The French Broad*, Wilma Dykeman lists a year's worth: "In March featherlike leaves of turkey corn are followed by its white queer-shaped blossoms from which a 'blood purifier' is made; then white blossoms of bloodroots, *sanguinaria*, used in treatment of bronchitis. Mandrake or May apple, then yellow ragwort, snakeroot and wild ginger that are mountain tonics, with the cohoshes used to control nervous disorders such as St. Vitus's dance. In May the delicate lady's-slippers glow pink and yellow in soft-mulched woods, and Indian hemp, used in treatment of Bright's disease and dropsy, follows the fringe bush; in midsummer come Indian tobacco and common Jimson and pokeweeds used to combat asthma; and in late summer the heather-colored boneset, for colds and fevers, fringes gullies and swamps. The balm of Gilead (or 'gilly b'am'), ingredient of healing ointments, especially for earache, is left for winter. Then also the fronds of ferns are gathered, boiled and used as remedy for colds and whooping cough." Knowledge of many of these remedies came from the Cherokee.

One of nature's commodities changed life in the Blue Ridge forever. In Georgia in July of 1829 a few nuggets of gold turned up in Ward's Creek, a branch of the Chestatee River. The discovery meant riches for a few, prosperity for many, and calamity for the Cherokee. Thousands of gold seekers squatted on Cherokee land in the southern Blue Ridge and immediately began agitating for confiscation of their territory. Andrew Jackson, now President—he who had fought gratefully alongside Cherokee warriors a number of times—supported efforts to remove the Indians. With his endorsement, the state of Georgia enacted laws confiscating Indian land, nullifying Indian law, and prohibiting Indian assembly. The Supreme Court, under John Marshall, declared Georgia's laws against the Cherokee unconstitutional, and the Indians and their supporters thought they had won. But Jackson, defying the Court, said, "John Marshall has made his decision. Now let him enforce it," and plans for Indian relocation proceeded.

A treaty railroaded through Congress and endorsed by just one-tenth of the Cherokee ceded to the U. S. all the eastern territory of the Indians for five million dollars and a comparable amount of land in the Oklahoma Territory. In the summer of 1838, Gen. Winfield Scott began the removal of the Indians. Soldiers rounded them up and herded them into stockades. Roaming bands of outlaws plundered their homes as soon as they were vacated. The trek to Oklahoma began in the autumn, with 13 detachments of about a thousand each, accompanied by wagons. They might have made it but for the early winter. Hundreds—then hundreds more—died of exposure and hunger as they trudged westward, and by the time they reached Oklahoma in March 1839 about 4,000 of them—almost a third of their original number—had died.

Back in the Blue Ridge, several hundred who had escaped the roundup took refuge in the mountains and managed to survive the winter. Eventually they would win the right to settle on a reservation in North Carolina—the Qualla Reservation, now the Cherokee Indian Reservation. Known as the Eastern Band, they live now in and around the town of Cherokee at the edge of the Smokies. Their craftspeople produce some of the country's finest baskets, pottery, beadwork, finger weavings, and stone and wood carvings.

As for the gold, 858,000 ounces were mined from the hills and streams around Dahlonega, Georgia, between 1880 and 1933. More is being mined today, but largely from the tourists who pass through this part of the Blue Ridge. "Gold's gold," a former miner said to me. Then he thought a minute and added, "Gold's *money*."

I took a seat one day on the porch of another former miner, Robert Jenkins, then 72, on the outskirts of Dahlonega. The house is a few yards off the highway, down the slope of a cool and shady ravine. Trestles beneath a low roof hold sluice boxes filled with water. Here tourists can stop, buy a pan of local dirt and gravel, and pan for its gold in the water—two dollars per pan. Mr. Jenkins is overalled and plump, with thin white hair.

"My grandfather was a gold miner," he told me, as birds chirped overhead. "One of the places he mined gold was right up there on the square in Dahlonega. Course there wasn't many people here way back then. Then my father mined for gold, and two uncles, they all mined. I started helping when I was a kid. Been in it ever since. My father, now. You wanted to pan careful if you was with him. If he come along behind you and scooped up a pan and found gold, he'd know you wasn't doin' it right.

"We had sluice boxes and stamp mills, all like that. A stamp mill crushes the rock so fine you wouldn't believe it. We had it both ways here, what they call placer mining.

"Dahlonega is on a gold belt that runs plumb on up through North Carolina, maybe to Alabama, I'm not for certain. You can find gold on that belt, but if you get off it, you can't find it."

Two young men from Germany, tourists, interrupt our talk. They want to pan for gold. Their English is minimal, and they communicate mostly with their hands. Robert gets a pan of dirt from the trunk of his car, shows them how to pan it, finds some gold, sells them each a pan of dirt, and they go happily to work, splashing up to their elbows in the water.

"You know gold from here went to Atlanta for the dome of the state capitol. Twice. Smog and stuff wrecked the first one. Seems like last time was maybe 60 ounces. Lots of gold."

Is the gold all gone, I ask.

"I'd speculate that a third of it's been taken out of the ground. It's getting harder. Landowners today don't want no holes dug. They want to develop their land for houses. You can walk over a place time after time and not know gold's there underground. These metal detectors, they pick up a certain amount that's near the surface. There's plenty of gold left here.

"The way it would work, you'd offer a landowner a percentage of the gold you'd find on his land. There were people who would try to cheat you. They'd wait 'til you'd found some gold, then hurry to the landowner and offer a bigger percentage. After you'd done the work of finding the gold. There was one guy who used to follow my father everywhere he went. Then he'd run back to the landowner and offer a bigger percentage.

"I was with my father one day when I was a tiny little fellow, and I never dreamed that my father had a gun. Farthest thing from my mind. We were goin' down a little bitty narrow trail, and Father kept looking back. This fella was coming along behind us. Father said, 'Let's walk fast,' and we went around a horseshoe bend, and he says, 'Let's stop right here.' So here come that fella, and my father come up with that gun, I swear it looked *that* long, and he told that man, 'You followed me. Now goddam you, you get back toward town or I'm gonna blow your goddam head off and leave you right here.' Boy! You talk about a man a-leavin'! My heart was in my mouth. I was so afraid my father was gonna shoot that man."

Guns had played a bloody part in the history of the Blue Ridge. Drive south from Front Royal, Virginia, in the Shenandoah Valley, and you find yourself on Stonewall Jackson Memorial Highway; you know you're not in Massachusetts. The Civil War came to the Blue Ridge and to the Great Valley with a vengeance. Its wounds can still be found. A docent at the Wilderness Road Regional Museum in Newbern, Virginia, tells of a small Civil War battle fought nearby. "We lost," she says.

The mountainous regions of North Carolina and Tennessee, far to the south, were solidly opposed to secession and, though geographically a part of the Confederacy, provided perhaps 50,000 Union soldiers in the conflict. And the northwestern part of Virginia—which snuggles up against the western flank of the Blue Ridge—broke away to become West Virginia and sent 30,000 troops into the Union Army.

Up and down the Shenandoah Valley, Confederate Gen. Stonewall Jackson, with relatively few men, kept 50,000 Union forces occupied throughout the spring of 1862, and a year later, Gen. Robert E. Lee led his force up the Shenandoah Valley on the road to Gettysburg. In the autumn of 1864, Union Gen. Philip Sheridan reduced the Shenandoah Valley—"the granary of the Confederacy"—to smoky ruin so the Rebels couldn't use it for resupply. The town of Winchester, Virginia, at the northern end of the valley, reportedly changed hands 72 times during the conflict. For years after the war, the mountains of North Carolina were filled with bitterness and resentment over the activities of "bushwhackers"—partisans on both sides of the conflict who had made life terrifying for mountaineers. Bloody skirmishes fought there between Union and Rebel guerrilla forces engendered feelings that remain hard to this day.

A regiment that was composed largely of Cherokee Indians, Thomas's Legion, remained loyal to the Confederacy and helped control the passes through the Great Smoky Mountains and along the French Broad River.

Jackson's Valley Campaign is talked about as if it had happened last year. His tactics and strategy are still studied at West Point, and the whole campaign is considered to have been a masterful example of military prowess. Historians praise especially his use of topography, interior lines, and the marching and fighting ability of his men as he played hide-and-seek with Union forces around Massanutten Mountain, a 45-mile-long monadnock lying between the North and South Forks of the Shenandoah River. He was a victim of what we now would call "friendly fire," fatally wounded by his own men at the Battle of Chancellorsville in 1863. His dying words were, "Let us cross over the river and rest under the shade of the trees."

General Lee ended his days at Lexington, as president of Washington College, which became Washington and Lee after his death in 1870. The text for his funeral sermon was, "Mark the perfect man, and behold the upright, for the end of that man is peace." He's buried in the Lee Chapel in Lexington.

Other Lexington boys—the cadets at the Virginia Military Institute, most of them teenagers, some as young as 15 years of age— won lasting renown at the Battle of New Market. Confederate Gen. John C. Breckinridge, outnumbered by Union forces, sent out a call for reinforcements, and the 257 cadets at VMI answered, marching for four days in the rain and mud to help assure a Confederate victory at New Market.

Reenactors gather each year in May to restage the Battle of New Market in a day of smoke and heat and thunderous artillery. As a crowd gathers, platoons and companies of soldiers—some in blue, some in gray—assemble. Fifes and drums sound "Dixie" and "Old Dan Tucker." Smaller squads of soldiers march to and fro, rifles on their shoulders. At the edge of the parade ground, three rows of tents shade merchants offering for sale the paraphernalia of reenactment: every kind of uniform button and all sorts of bullets, rifles, hats, dresses, musket slings, lead soldiers, officers' uniforms, shoulder patches for every outfit, even a newspaper published just for reenactors. In it are listed more than a hundred upcoming reenactments around the country. There are ads for Sibley Camp Stoves and the Rapidan River Canteen Company. An article laments the fact that most reenactors want to be Confederates, so it's difficult to get the forces' proportions right. A sign on one of the tents hawks "musket slings, nipples, and wonder wads."

In a moist cove near Sylva, North Carolina, Lee Crites cultivates ginseng. Mountain people call the root "sang." Traditionally they sold it to raise cash to pay taxes. They also boiled the root and drank sang tea to soothe arthritis. The Cherokee sold large amounts of ginseng to traders who sent it to the Orient. The Chinese still prize Blue Ridge sang as an aphrodisiac. Some scientists claim that ginseng can be beneficial; others warn that it may be dangerous. "Sang pullers" like Lee are licensed by their state.

When the reenactment begins, bystanders in shorts and T-shirts crowd as close to the action as they can. Children scream and babies cry at the noise and confusion. People farther back in the crowd can't see much, just swords being waved over the heads of officers charging on horseback. Cannon make smoke rings in the sky, and the ground shakes. When the temperature on the treeless hilltop reaches 91°, people start heading for the parking lot.

On another hot day, alone, I visited New Market to walk through the actual battlefield, now a historic park. The gnats are troublesome, and the apples look ready for picking in the orchard of the Bushong farm, which got caught in the middle of the battle. Tiny grasshoppers dodge my feet. I pause at Woodson's Missouri Monument and read: "This rustic pile a simple tale will tell; it marks the spot where Woodson's heroes fell."

A grassy path has been mowed along the route of the walking tour. I hear, high overhead, the murmur of a jet; what would the cadets make of that? They charged across this field in the mud and later dubbed it the Field of Lost Shoes. Scrambling over a fence, one recalled: "As I surmounted the topmost rail, I felt at least ten feet up in the air and the special object of hostile aim." The night before the battle, General Breckinridge had said to them, "Gentlemen, . . . I trust you will do your duty." I find myself walking toward a cannon that's aimed squarely at me, and I'm not certain I could do *my* duty if I knew it was about to fire.

In the museum is a touching letter from a 19-year-old cadet to his mother dated May 12, three days before the battle. The telegram telling of his death reached her on May 16, before the letter. Over 50 of his classmates also died or were wounded at New Market.

I t was in Front Royal that I found evidence of my favorite Civil War character: *La Belle Rebelle*, the Cleopatra of the Secession, the Joan of Arc of the South, the Siren of the Shenandoah— Belle Boyd. Contemporary accounts speak of her as plain but charming, "spunky," and possessing a zest for adventure. Though an amateurish spy, she managed to be troublesome to the Yankees, acting as courier and messenger. (To one Yankee she was worse than troublesome, shooting him dead when he entered her home in Martinsburg, insulting her mother "in language as offensive as it is possible to conceive.")

She shocked her friends by flirting with soldiers both blue and gray, by visiting military camps, by calling on generals and colonels in their tents, by going for rides with enemy officers and soldiers. All in the line of duty, she said. She spent some time in prison in Washington, D.C., charged with being a Confederate spy. A visitor found her there "reading *Harpers* and eating peaches." Her father kept moving her around—from Winchester to Front Royal to Martinsburg—trying to keep her out of trouble, but she seemed always to be in the thick of things. She made midnight rides to warn Stonewall Jackson of troop movements, and once, in Front Royal, ran on foot through the advancing Rebels, with bullets flying around her, to get a message to Jackson. He thanked her, she said, with a note praising her "immense service," though the note was never seen by anyone but Belle.

In Front Royal she lived in a cottage behind a hotel run by her aunt and uncle, and there found occasion to listen, in an upstairs closet, through a hole in the floor to Yankees making plans in the parlor below. Though the hotel is gone and the hole in the floor with it, the cottage exists still.

Magretta Biggs, of the Warren Heritage Society, showed me through the four-room building. Brightly painted walls downstairs, a handsome old bed upstairs, a second-day wedding dress, "for wearing the day after the wedding," some clippings and photos of Belle. I observed that she wasn't really very pretty, for a femme fatale. "No," said Magretta, "I guess she wasn't. And in those days they didn't have much . . . help." A friendly puppy named Sam brought me a piece of an old slipper, then wagged his tail.

Belle married three times, had a successful career on the stage giving dramatic monologues about her wartime exploits, and died in Wisconsin in 1900, still touring.

"There is, perhaps, no tract of country in the world more lovely than the Valley of the Shenandoah," Belle wrote. The valley and the river both end just to the north of Front Royal at Harpers Ferry. The little town has had its share of excitement. Floods periodically sweep through, climbing to second story windows. Here the Shenandoah, having gathered its North and South Forks together at Front Royal, joins with the Potomac to sunder the Blue Ridge. Thomas Jefferson thought the view of the confluence worth a trip across the Atlantic. Here John Brown staged his fearsome raid on a federal armory, contributing his particular thunderbolt to the gathering storm of the Civil War.

On Labor Day weekend I visited Harpers Ferry—the historic section of it now run by the National Park Service—and found the streets full of ladies in hoopskirts and reenactors in heavy wool uniforms. A preschooler, viewing the tents of the reenactors, begged his father: "I wanna live in a tent." One of the uniformed soldiers was wearing an earring.

The day was as hot as John Brown's fury. Crowds of steaming tourists strolled through the town, pausing to read signboards at the Blacksmith Shop, the Master Armorer's House, the John Brown Museum, Arsenal Square. Beneath the fierce sun I wilted badly, and a milkshake, almost too cold to hold, may have saved my life. Rafters, canoers, kayakers, swimmers—even dogs—splashed in the rivers. From the shallows, small flocks of Canada geese watched the passing flotillas.

The Blue Ridge Range here subsides like a sleeping giant, its aged and wrinkled body stretched back toward Georgia. Its old stories have been often told, its old hills climbed, its old songs sung:

In the sky the bright stars glittered,
On the bank the pale moon shone.
And 'twas from Aunt Dinah's quilting party
I was seeing Nellie home.

But there's life in these old hills yet, and to find it, what better place to start than with the land itself?

"I think that I shall never see / a poem lovely as a tree." This familiar refrain plays ever new in North Carolina's Joyce Kilmer-Slickrock Wilderness. Within the sanctuary, a huge tulip tree (right) guards a tract known as the Joyce Kilmer Memorial Forest. One of the last remaining stands of virgin woodland in the United States, the area honors the author who in 1913 wrote the poem "Trees." Rocky creeks full of trout lace the heavy forest, where native poplar, hemlock, and oak stretch to rare heights of more than 100 feet.

DAVID MUENCH

Talented hands of Louise Bigmeat Maney call on pottery skills perfected by her Cherokee ancestors. She presses designs into a clay pot with a cut-off spoon; her forebears, the Bigmeat family, would have used a stick or a peach pit. Early Cherokee excelled in weaving, carving, and pottery. Today most members of the tribe devote time to arts and crafts. John J. Wilnoty carved this chief's head (opposite) from oak. The burial urn (right), crafted by Louise, carries embellishments for the tourist trade, an important source of income for today's Cherokee.

Barker's Creek powers a gristmill near Dillard, Georgia, where the splash of the waterwheel sings of pioneer days. A showpiece of the Hambidge Center, an artists' colony, the mill today produces meal and grits. Laurence Holden pours corn into a hopper to be ground for local people. The "miller's toll"— one-eighth—is sold to visitors and mail-order customers.

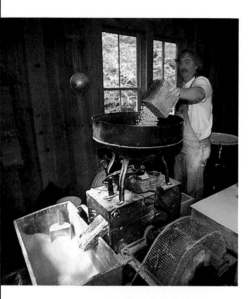

Sparks fly from blacksmith, shingle maker, and teacher of old skills Danny Wingate of Elk Creek, Virginia. Above, Danny takes a break from riving. With the mallet he will finish splitting logs into 20,000 shingles, to be used in the restoration of a Tennessee museum.

FOLLOWING PAGES: Flowing out of the Blue Ridge, the Potomac, at right, and the Shenandoah converge at Harpers Ferry. John Brown's raid on the arsenal here in 1859 heralded the Civil War.

Catawba rhododendrons blanket Roan Mountain slopes along the Tennessee-North Carolina border. The rich botanical diversity of the humid, cloud-caressed Blue Ridge has long intrigued botanists.

THE LAND

T HE BLUE RIDGE MOUNTAINS WERE OLD when the Himalaya were born, were ancient when the Alps erupted, were worn nearly to nubbins when the Rockies arose in the West. Their bedrock is among the oldest on earth, some of it dating from Precambrian and early Paleozoic times 1,100 million years ago. "The Blue Ridge is the heart of 'Old' Appalachia," writes Maurice Brooks in *The Appalachians*. There are few fossils in the Blue Ridge, though the mountains witnessed the age of reptiles; the heat and pressure of their formation destroyed most traces of life. And no glaciers touched these aged hills. Their smooth, rounded profiles result solely from the inexorable sculpting of weather and erosion.

The Blue Ridge is not a large mountain range. From Harpers Ferry to Dahlonega is a straight line of barely 500 miles, and a healthy hiker could walk across the mountains—from the Piedmont to the Great Valley—anywhere along its length in a day. Though strung out over those 500 miles, the mountains are botanically, geologically, and culturally one range.

Settlers moving upriver from the coast encountered the end of navigable water where waterfalls and rapids began. Here, at the fall line, cities arose. From the fall line upward, the foothills stairstep through the Piedmont to the mountains. Beyond the Blue Ridge to the west lies a broad region of lower folds called the valley and ridge province, and west of that are the Allegheny Mountains.

Water gaps—breaks in the mountains carved by rivers—cut the Blue Ridge repeatedly. At one time Indians and settlers moved slowly through them—Swift Run Gap, Ashby's Gap, Rockfish Gap, Buffalo Gap, the Roanoke Water Gap. Now highways do.

In the geography of the Blue Ridge, two features are common: coves and balds. A cove is a level area rimmed by mountains. Balds are large spots bare of trees on or near the mountain summits. They are enigmatic, and botanists can't explain them. Perhaps fires in the past so damaged the soil that trees can't grow; perhaps there's something in the wind and rain patterns that supports only grasses and shrubs; perhaps the grassy balds were kept open by the grazing livestock of settlers and will one day once again be tree covered.

So jumbled are these hills, so tangled their topography that travelers despair of finding a road that doesn't take twenty miles to go ten. Rivers often seem to be running the wrong direction—even uphill. Donald Culross Peattie wrote, "Every stream has a hundred tributaries, every tributary a hundred forks, every fork a thousand tiny streamlets. And all of them have their gullies, side ravines, little valleys and bigger valleys."

The complexity of the landscape itself slowed settlement. These mountains not only create the landscape; they also preserve it. The hills set the pace. Life here must always have been slow, especially in horse-and-buggy days. Slow talking, slow moving, slow-to-passion people evolved to populate them.

Rain comes often to the mountains. Flickers of lightning, rumbles of thunder—soon the roadsides are awash. Later, wisps of mist drift up the green slopes like smoke from explorers' fires. Streams fill up and turn angry and brown for an hour or two, then settle down.

Beneath the Blue Ridge lies a world as diverse, as intriguing,

Spring runoff cascades over moss-and-lichen-cloaked boulders at the edge of the Smokies. Hundreds of rivers and creeks thread these well-watered mountains. Deluges probably tumbled these huge rocks into the valley long ago. Now mosses—among some 400 species in the region— and lichens pioneer the barren rock surface, retaining moisture and gradually creating soil to support more complex plant life.

and as rich as that above ground. Caves and caverns in the soft limestone, carved over eons by slightly acidic groundwater dripping and seeping and moving, provide miles of underground exploration for cavers. There are more than 3,000 caves in Virginia alone, 19 of them commercial caverns in the Blue Ridge. Gary Berdeaux guided me through those his family has owned since 1984: Endless Caverns— so named because their end has yet to be reached. The entrance is near New Market, and they were opened to the public in 1920.

"Caverns here in the Shenandoah Valley began opening late in the 1800s," Gary told me. "The famous cavern at Luray opened a year or so before this one. The first owner here, Reuben Zirkle, learned to hijack customers. Trains arrived at the station in New Market full of people wanting to visit Luray, and Zirkle would go over there with a coach and yell, 'Stage to the cave!' and haul people up here."

It was cool and quiet in the cave, which we had to ourselves. Gary turned lights on and off as we progressed, past formations rising from the floor and others descending from the ceiling, past pools and puddles and miniature, upside-down Grand Canyons. In places, sooty stains marked the ceiling, from the days when people toured the cave by candlelight and lantern.

A lone brown bat, about the size and shape of a furry ping-pong ball, had tucked itself into a crevice on the ceiling. "He got in the same way you and I did—through the door," Gary said.

During the off-season, Gary and his brother Wade explore farther into the cave, mapping as they go. They have maps of about four and a half miles of underground passageways, quite a bit more than the mile or so that the tourists see. Gary showed me one of the maps, a three-dimensional maze. Minute symbols, like the tracks of tiny birds, covered the paper. "They're a shorthand for identifying the features of a cave," Gary said. "A dashed line that looks like a swamp on a surface map actually indicates mud. These little solid lines with tick marks indicate a drop-off—a cliff. The T symbols signify a change in the height of the cave. These little splayed chicken feet mark a slope."

Aboveground, rivers pattern the Blue Ridge like the veins of a long, thin leaf, tending either toward the Atlantic Ocean or the Gulf of Mexico. The Roanoke, the James, the Rapidan, the French Broad—above the fall line they led settlers into the mountains, where roads hacked in the wilderness took them beyond to the valleys of the eastern woodlands. The Potomac River makes a decisive end to the Blue Ridge in the north. The Shenandoah, in its North and South Forks, confines itself to its namesake valley for 150 miles, straddling Massanutten Mountain in its middle.

Once there were three Broad Rivers in the southern Appalachians; one ran into territory held by the French, so it became the French Broad River. It connects Asheville with Knoxville. The Cherokee called the river Long Man, and said Long Man's head was in the mountains, his feet in the valleys, and that he was fed by the "chattering children" of his tributary streams. For three quarters of a century, drovers herded livestock from the pastures of the south to the markets of the north along its rugged bank, passing with difficulty and ingenuity through the 70-odd miles of the French Broad Canyon. As many as 150,000 hogs a year, in noisy, smelly herds, went thus to market.

Only one river, the New, flows across the entire Blue Ridge, arising in western North Carolina. Eventually its waters join the Ohio River far away to the north in West Virginia. On its banks, near Austinville, Virginia, stands an old brick shot tower, where cannonballs were once manufactured. The tower is protected now in a state park, and at its base a trail runs alongside the river.

I t's perfectly flat, an old railroad bed, fine for walking, so I pick a warm summer day and walk it. A steep bluff rises on the left and the wide New River slides past on the right. Within just a hundred yards or so, the roar and clatter of traffic on Interstate 77 fade, and quiet descends.

The New River, called by one geologist "the master stream of a primeval America," is one of the oldest rivers on the planet. It originated during an upheaval of the Appalachians, survived their gradual destruction, and held its own against the most recent upheaval. It has seemed to many people—as it seems to me—to be running in a contrary direction. At one point near the North Carolina-Virginia border, the New River runs—incredibly—at nearly right angles to the wall of the Blue Ridge, *toward* the mountains.

As I walk, chipmunks chitter from the bluff. Tufted titmice flit through the trees. I round a bend and come to noisy ripples in the river, as it drops over shallow shelves. Bank swallows skim across its surface. Highway 52 is across the river, but there's not much traffic on it. I pass a small concrete pillar with P26 on it; presumably a mile marker. Soon there's another one: P27. After an hour I come upon a bench, so sit down to eat my Nature's Wafers Oatbran Bar, and a family—Mom, Dad, Sis—go past on mountain bikes. Crows are cawing somewhere, and a jet hums past far overhead—the two sounds you can almost always hear in an eastern forest.

Suddenly there's a big field of red peppers between me and the river, and with my binoculars I watch a rabbit come out of the field and pause on the trail. I meet three teenagers, two girls and a boy, with a puppy on a leash, and pass abandoned buildings, an old log house and a newer one with a barn. I come to a bridge with a sign: "Warning. Please Dismount and Lead Horse Across Trestle"—a sign with nice manners. Beyond the bridge, I come to a tunnel, an unusual experience on foot. Its opening is shaped like a slice of bread. There's another sign: "Warning. Please Dismount and Lead Horse Through Tunnel." All this talk of horses makes me wish I had one. The walls of the tunnel are jagged from blasting.

The area I'm walking along would be under water now if the Appalachian Power Company had got its way. In the sixties the utility proposed a hydroelectric facility here, the Blue Ridge Project. It would have created two reservoirs of more than 42,000 acres that would have inundated 893 homes, 41 summer cabins, 10 industrial establishments, 23 commercial facilities, 5 post offices, 15 churches, and 12 cemeteries. Nearly 3,000 people would have had to move. The power would have gone to urban areas of the East and Midwest. A group of politicians, New River Valley residents, conservationists, and journalists needed 11 years to get the project killed.

Coming out of the tunnel, I hear hammering across the river and through my binoculars I see two men and a boy building a deck on the back of a house. Suddenly five or six turkey vultures are soaring overhead, and I wonder if it's me they're watching. They don't flap their wings, but circle and circle. A female cardinal sits in a berry bush and watches me go by. A gust of wind makes a handful of dry leaves fall; they clatter as they descend through the trees. I hear a squeaking behind me and turn to find an elderly man on a bicycle gaining on me. His doctor has ordered him to ride a couple of miles a day for his rheumatic knees. He sees a lot of deer, he says, and once saw a bear track. Ahead there's a bridge—where Virginia Route 619 crosses the river—and soon I'm there. A signboard along the highway welcomes me to New River Trail State Park, "Virginia's only linear state park." It will be 57 miles long when completed.

The Blue Ridge is famous for its forests. That fictional hiker—the one who could walk across the Blue Ridge in a day—would make, in biological, climatological, and zoological terms, a trek through forests as varied as if he had walked from Georgia to central Quebec. He would pass from Piedmont woods through hardwood groves to spruce-fir forests in the upper elevations. He would come across many of the 130 species of trees, the 1,400 species of flowering herbs, the 350 species of mosses and related plants, and the 2,000 species of fungi that grow in the Blue Ridge.

At lower elevations, the Piedmont woods reach up valleys and blanket the Asheville Plateau. Trees here—oak, hickory, pine, tulip, and maple—are early to leaf in the spring and late to shed their leaves in the fall. They're often called "scrub forests" by mountain people. Up a step, between elevations of 2,000 and 4,000 feet, there grows a transition zone, composed of many of the trees that appear both above and below it. It constitutes the great mass of forest that visitors see while driving through the Blue Ridge. Higher still are the northern hardwoods—maple, beech, white oak, cherry—a forest group that is almost entirely naked in winter. And on top, on the windswept ridges and high, north-facing slopes, grows the spruce-fir forest. In effect, the north woods.

In 1888 there came to the forests of North Carolina a man who would change them profoundly—would change the forests of the entire country, in fact. George Washington Vanderbilt, enormously wealthy scion of New York's Vanderbilt family, visited Asheville that year and, entranced with the climate and the mountains, began purchasing tracts of land on and around Mount Pisgah. Eventually his holdings there totaled 125,000 acres.

He constructed a magnificent estate, Biltmore, to rival the grand country houses of Europe. He hired the renowned Frederick Law Olmsted to landscape the estate and Gifford Pinchot to manage the vast forest properties. Pinchot had never seen such a variety of marketable trees. "I'm not here to stay the ax, but to modify it," he said, and set men to work selectively harvesting trees. He left Biltmore in 1898, appointed chief of the new U.S. Forest Service by

As if to wash its paws, a young raccoon dips into Abrams Creek in eastern Tennessee. The animal more likely is hunting for a fish or a frog to eat. Called Aroughcun— or "he scratches with his hands"—by the Cherokee, the canny omnivore thrives in these mountains.

BILL LEA

Theodore Roosevelt, and his replacement was Dr. Carl Albert Schenck, a German forester. To instruct the seven young foresters he hired to assist him in trail building, fire fighting, planting, and marking, Dr. Schenck in 1898 established the first forestry school in the U.S., the Biltmore Forest School, on the grounds of the estate. It survived until 1914, and for the next generation its 367 alumni worked as professional foresters throughout the country.

In 1968, some 6,400 acres of the Pisgah National Forest— where Dr. Schenck had his school—were set aside by Congress as the Cradle of Forestry. A couple of trails meander through the grounds, past the little schoolhouse where the students gathered for lectures, past a typical ranger's cabin, past displays that tell the story of early forestry practices, past a 1900 portable steam-powered sawmill and a restored 1915 Climax logging locomotive.

The mountain laurel was abloom in lovely profusion the day I visited, and the trails were banked with beds of its delicate pink and white blossoms. Various craftspeople demonstrate their skills here and there around the grounds, and I stopped to talk for a minute with blacksmith David Woolley. He was making fireplace utensils. I admired the intricate patterns he was creating. I said I was always surprised at the things you could do with metal when you got it hot. "You either make it or break it," he said.

On the porch of the Black Forest Lodge, a structure typical of several built throughout the forest by Schenck as residences for his rangers, were boxes of bright red geraniums. Nearby, toymaker Bob Miller, in suspenders as red as the geraniums, was making wooden toys. He set a walnut top to spinning. "This old floor don't make a very good place to spin it," he said. He demonstrated a limberjack— "a toy that originated in the Appalachian Mountains." It was a small wooden figure of a man, his joints hinged and loose, that dangled so that just his feet touched a flexible board. Bob made him dance, even—astonishingly—made him moonwalk backward like Michael Jackson. "Here's the one that brings back memories to anybody over 40 years old—the button on the string." Indeed it did. Bob taught me to operate a whimmy-diddle: a tiny propeller nailed to the end of a rhododendron twig. Rub the twig with another piece of rhododendron, and the propeller spins. Hold your thumb a little differently, and you can make the propeller reverse direction.

These Blue Ridge Mountains have long attracted naturalists. William Bartram wandered through the southern Appalachians in 1775, recording black oaks with trunks 30 feet around, beeches and sweet gums 150 feet tall, and chestnuts 13 feet thick at the base. A "sublime forest," he thought it. André Michaux came in 1802, collecting plants for the gardens of Versailles.

Donald Culross Peattie wrote of the great naturalists in *Green Laurels* and was himself a careful observer of the Blue Ridge. The range's disparate salamanders, famous among zoologists, intrigued him. "The salamanders," he wrote one March, "have crept out to mate, in that detached, cool-blooded way of theirs. . . . I have said that much of life and perhaps the best of it is not quite 'nice.' The business of early spring is not; it transpires in nakedness and candor, under high empty skies."

Annie Dillard, who lived in the Blue Ridge near Roanoke, celebrated the mountains—and much more—in *Pilgrim at Tinker Creek,* uncovering enigmas and plumbing theological mysteries in the natural world. "The mountains—Tinker and Brushy, McAfee's Knob and Dead Man—are a passive mystery, the oldest of all," she wrote. "Mountains are giant, restful, absorbent. You can heave your spirit into a mountain and the mountain will keep it, folded."

Parts of seven national forests, their boundaries notoriously helter-skelter, sprawl across the Blue Ridge. They were established after the turn of the century, largely for watershed protection and logging. They all provide work for loggers and lumber for builders and pulp mills, recreation for hikers and fishermen and hunters, and days in the woods for families of picnickers. The national forests of North Carolina alone attracted 34 million visitors in 1990.

Jim Kidd, a thoughtful young forester with the Chattahoochee National Forest in Georgia, gave me a lift one day to a work site in the forest, where the Forest Service, the Georgia Appalachian Trail Club, and a local builder—Upper Loft Design—were collaborating on the construction of a new shelter on the Appalachian Trail. "Upper Loft holds timber-framing workshops," Jim told me, "and people come from around the country to learn that old construction technique. They're always on the lookout for a project to build. This way everyone gets something: *(Continued on page 64)*

Promontory of Looking Glass Rock emerges above a mantle of trees, once part of George Vanderbilt's 125,000-acre Biltmore estate and now in Pisgah National Forest. The rock face—left behind after softer rock layers eroded—derives its name from its glistening appearance when winter coats it with ice or when spring rains gleam on its surface. At Biltmore, in 1898, the country's first forestry school opened under the direction of German forester Carl A. Schenck. He writes of an excursion of guests from Biltmore: "We climbed to the top of Lookingglass Rock on a series of rustic ladders." Today's climbers find the going tougher, inching their way up the exposed 500-foot granite expanse.

Between a rock and a hard place, rafters slide into "Jawbone," one of the most difficult rapids on the Chattooga. A kayaker braves another frothing chute on the river, which forms some 40 miles of the Georgia-South Carolina border. The Chattooga's wild gorge set the scene for the movie based on James Dickey's novel, Deliverance. "I prayed that there would be no rapids while we were in the gorge," says Dickey's narrator, "or that they would be easy ones." After the movie's release, inexperienced boaters had no such qualms, and many drowned here in some of the most challenging white water in the Southeast. Now the U.S. Forest Service administers river use for some 70,000 visitors a year.

Raising the roof, a crew of apprentice timber framers eases a gable end, or bent, into place. Old ways serve new needs along the Blue Ridge: Upper Loft Design teaches traditional timber-frame techniques in cooperation with the Forest Service and the Appalachian Trail Club to construct a new shelter on the trail at Deep Gap, in Georgia's Chattahoochee National Forest. An apprentice uses a sledgehammer to nudge a post into alignment. Wooden pegs and mortise-and-tenon joinery serve in place of nails.

Getting a jump on spring, a "thru-hiker" trudges northward in mid-March in the Chattahoochee, at the beginning of his 2,000-mile journey along the Appalachian Trail. Two other hikers camp at the Deep Gap shelter. Footpaths that once served Indians and settlers in this convoluted region now offer recreational opportunities. The Blue Ridge salamander (right) emerges later in the spring in North Carolina's Nantahala National Forest. Variations in elevation and rainfall in these mountains have created ecological niches for a wide range of animal and plant species—often endemics, which survive only in limited areas.

Outcroppings of gneiss rise beyond a sprawl of mountain ash on 5,964-foot Grandfather Mountain, one of the highest peaks in the Blue Ridge. Controversy swirls around the massive ridge, as developers confront conservationists here in western North Carolina. Carolina rhododendrons cling to the crags of nearby Linville Gorge, protected by wilderness status.

FOLLOWING PAGES: The eastern mountain lion probably survives in the wild only in the imagination—although sightings are occasionally reported. This female lives in a wildlife habitat on Grandfather Mountain.

Forested uplands of Panthertown Valley stretch to the horizon in the Nantahala National Forest. So taken was botanist William Bartram with the Blue Ridge landscape that he nearly overlooked "the assembly of mountain beauties" at his feet. He and his father,

WHITE AZALEA
YELLOW FRINGED ORCHIS (LEFT)

CRESTED DWARF IRIS

John, described more than a score of new plant species, including the flame azalea. Spring and summer bring a colorful succession of flowers. Deep, fertile soils, plentiful moisture, and varied terrain have produced in the Blue Ridge a vast diversity of flora.

FLAME AZALEA

FIRE PINK
BUTTERFLY WEED (RIGHT)

the Forest Service gets a new shelter in the Chattahoochee National Forest at a greatly reduced cost; the folks at Upper Loft get a project for their students to work on; and the GATC gets a fine new shelter as well as a weekend, hands-on project for its members. There'll be a lot of them there today to help put this thing up."

Jim talked with me about the impact the national forest has on local communities. "Many people here in Rabun County make their living from logging," he said, "and they lose patience with people who move up here and think the only thing these trees are good for is recreation. This huge influx of second-home people we're getting, largely from Florida—they don't understand multiple use, which is what the Forest Service is all about.

"Being a forester, I look at things in terms of a hundred years. I know the history here. I know that large sections across 40,000 acres here were clear-cut in the thirties. Now you've got a brand-new forest. People from outside see we've harvested a 20-acre plot, and they say, 'Oh, you've destroyed it.'

"Another big impact on our forests: the flood of people coming up from Atlanta on weekends. They congregate in about 5 percent of the forest, and we have to try to mitigate that impact. I think logging will become a smaller and smaller proportion of the county's income as recreation becomes more important.

"Rabun County is oddly apportioned as it is: About 60 percent of the county is in the Chattahoochee National Forest, about 10 percent belongs to Georgia Power, and only that final 30 percent is private. So anything the national forest does has tremendous impact on local people, on their economy, and on recreation."

We were nearing our destination, bouncing along a narrow, rutted gravel road that wound up and down through the forest, which came right to the edge of the road. Forest service campgrounds appeared at intervals, crowded with weekend campers. "This is Wildcat Creek Road," Jim said, "built by the Civilian Conservation Corps—the CCC. It has had 60 years of constant use, with not much money spent on it. In the last 20 years, there's been very little maintenance. It's about gone."

The Forest Service has been criticized by environmentalists for building too many roads through its forests, for bisecting potential wilderness areas, for catering too eagerly to logging companies by easing access to stands of timber. "We're still getting a lot of criticism for that," said Jim. "But now probably 90 percent of the access roads that we build are temporary. After an area is logged, we'll close the road and seed it down. It was in the sixties and seventies that the road building increased so greatly. In the last ten years things have changed. People who grew up in the sixties and are more environmentally aware are beginning to advance cautiously into positions of authority in the Forest Service."

Wildcat Creek Road came to a dead end alongside a steep bank. Standing around were a couple dozen people—Forest Service employees, hikers from the GATC, apprentice builders from Upper Loft. We began hauling tools, equipment, and supplies up the hill a hundred yards or so to the site of the new shelter. Dogs and children scurried back and forth, and squirrels retreated to the treetops. The huge beams and timbers, precut by the apprentices at the Upper

Loft shop, weighed hundreds of pounds apiece and were carried, centipede-like, by men grunting and sweating up the slippery slope. Soon the timber framers had their timbers down on the ground and were hammering them together with wooden pegs.

I found John Koenig, owner of Upper Loft, and asked him about timber framing. "My father was a timber carpenter," he said. "He came from Germany, discovered two-by-fours and nails, and joined the carpenters' union in upstate New York. He got me into a carpentry apprenticeship right out of high school."

Wooden buildings today are raised around a frame of two-by-fours, he told me, but before the invention of nails, structures were built of heavy posts and beams. The posts were the uprights, and the beams connected and gave stability to the posts. Braces ran between them, providing strength and firmness. Intricately crafted joints—the most common is the mortise and tenon—held the whole thing solidly together. Buildings made this way can stand hundreds of years.

"In the mid-seventies, there began a revival of interest in timber framing," said John. "We've been building timber-frame homes around northeastern Georgia since about 1985. At first my dad was opposed to it. Typical old-world attitude. He thought we wouldn't to be able to make a go of it. Now he's real excited."

The warm, sunny day was perfect for raising a barn—or an AT shelter. By early afternoon, the workmen had all their posts and beams pegged together. The assembled end pieces—called bents—each weighed 2,500 pounds, so it called for cooperation from all hands, for careful coordination of pushing and pulling, for a system of tethers and guy lines to get the massive things upright and steady. By late afternoon, when we dispersed, a frame that looked solid enough to last a thousand years stood, awaiting only a roof and some siding. A new penny was placed under the number-one corner post, a tradition, and all the workers clambered up onto the rafters for a group photo.

Hikers on the Appalachian Trail are pretty well assured of a degree of solitude, but solitude is becoming rare in this section of the Blue Ridge. Retirement homes and communities are proliferating, as Jim had told me. One cause: Florida has overflowed. John Duncan, whose great-great-grandfather was one of the first white settlers in Rabun County, talked with me one day in his home in Franklin, North Carolina. "In a nutshell—" he said.

"*Nut*-shell!" interrupted his four-year-old son, John Harper.

"In a nutshell," persisted John, "the trouble began back in the sixties. Getting a broker's license was made as easy as possible. Presto! You're a real estate agent. People here got the notion that they could get rich selling off the old homestead.

"At the same time, Florida filled up and got badly overpriced. People there found they could sell their condo for $250,000 and come up here to north Georgia or southern North Carolina, buy fifty acres of prime mountain real estate, divide it up into little five-acre plots, and make a lot of money. And people here were eager to sell. They thought their land was only good for ranging hogs and cattle and selling a little timber, maybe for some hunting. They couldn't see what anybody would want with this land. They thought they were really putting something over on the city slickers.

"Later, in the seventies and eighties, when junk money was plentiful, the big boom in development began. Every hustler who wanted to could come in here, call himself a developer, and start throwing up cheap subdivisions." The new developments attracted even more newcomers, often people whose attitudes offended the locals. "Many, having moved to Florida from somewhere else, were now moving from Florida to the Blue Ridge and were thus two steps removed from any sense of 'home.'

"They brought in No Trespassing signs and biting dogs," said John. "They came up here and immediately established the Florida Club."

A side effect of this new development is a problem met up and down the Blue Ridge: As property values rise, so do taxes, and locals can no longer afford their own land. Absentee landlords become the norm. "At the Rabun Gap School," said John, "many children come from families that do not own their own homes. Most of the tax bills of Rabun County are mailed out of state."

Shoddy development and environmentally unsound practices have resulted. In the past, the wealthy town of Highlands, North Carolina—begun as a mountain retreat after the Civil War—outraged homeowners downstream by dumping sewage into the scenic Cullasaja River. Now, a state-of-the-art treatment facility has largely allayed these concerns.

And near Banner Elk, a 12-story condominium built squarely on a ridge line is visible for miles in every direction, destroying the "view-shed" of thousands of people. I drove up to the ridgetop to get a closer look one day, and jotted down the signs I passed by: Warning. Private Property. No Trespassing. Property Owners and Rentals Must Register at the Homeowners' Association. Parking by Permit Only. Admission Only for Owners, Guests, Renters, and Restaurant Patrons. The building seemed as large as an aircraft carrier, and as out of place. It, at least, led to the passage of so-called "ridge laws" that prevent more such structures from being built.

"Coming soon," I read on a roadside sign in North Carolina, "Joyce Kilmer Golf and Country Club."

I f the forests of the Blue Ridge are under attack by people who love them too much, there are other, more immediate threats: pests and diseases such as the blight that has eliminated the American chestnut from the Blue Ridge.

"One day we'll have large chestnut trees in the Blue Ridge again," Dr. Wayne T. Swank told me. "I feel certain of it." Dr. Swank is Project Leader of the Coweeta Hydrologic Laboratory, a few miles north of Clayton, Georgia. It is one of several Forest Service outdoor sites to carry the "laboratory" designation. The 5,400-acre laboratory, in operation for more than 50 years, measures the amounts and timing of rainfall, evaporation, and stream flow in the forest. About a hundred graduate students and scientists conduct research projects in the numerous small watersheds on the site.

"The ecosystems here are extremely stable, extremely resilient," said Dr. Swank. "They recover rapidly. As you drove up the basin to get here, you were looking right into an area that's been

Prolific intruders, kudzu vines drape trees along a North Carolina road. The exotic plant, introduced into the U.S. from the Orient in the late 1800s, grows a much as a foot a day. Kudzu can threaten less rapacious, slower-growing native flora.

clear-cut twice in the last 50 years, yet you can't see it. These hills have been burned, been grazed, been farmed, been logged—yet look at how beautiful and healthy they are. I would argue that if ever we could have a place in the world where we can have our cake and eat it too, it's in ecosystems like this."

The dogwood tree, perhaps the loveliest symbol of the Blue Ridge Mountains, is under attack from dogwood anthracnose, a fungus. "Anthracnose was first noticed in New York and Connecticut in 1978," said Dr. Swank. Within ten years the disease had moved south to the Catoctin Mountains in Maryland; by that year, 89 percent of the dogwoods around the presidential retreat at Camp David were dead." Now it's here, and a topic of our research. It appears to thrive best at higher elevations, in cool, wet coves. Open, sunny locations seem to reduce its spread."

"We're also doing some research here on the loss of the chestnut," Dr. Swank told me, "on what's replacing it, on what its loss has meant to the wildlife population. We get a lot of natural re-sprouting—trees get about five inches in diameter and then the blight gets them. Some trees even produce a crop of nuts. A few survive simply by chance. The spores don't happen to reach them."

At one time perhaps 25 percent of the Appalachian forest was made up of the American chestnut, and ridgetops were often pure chestnut. Trees could live 600 years and rise 80 to 100 feet. Street vendors in eastern cities sold the roasted nuts, and cooks at holiday time used them to stuff roast goose and turkey. Chestnut trees provided lumber for construction, telegraph poles, railroad ties, even furniture, and were the major source of tannin for tanning leather. But the blight that struck in 1904 needed only 50 years to kill virtually every chestnut tree in the U.S.

Donald Culross Peattie remembered a day in the early 1900s when he looked out from Mount Mitchell "upon the whole forest, far as eye could see, tossing with the creamy blooms of the chestnut. . . . Each crown bore such a myriad of long shining catkins, that as the wind threshed those woods the whole sea of waving leaves seemed breaking into whitecaps."

The American chestnut is being inched back toward health at

a number of places. In southern Virginia, near the village of Meadowview, the American Chestnut Foundation supports a research farm under the direction of Dr. Frederick V. Hebard. I walked with him around the 20-acre site, where some 2,500 young trees are tended. The attempt here: Crossbreed the American chestnut with the blight-resistant Chinese chestnut, back and back, until you have a tree that's maybe 15/16ths American chestnut and 1/16th Chinese chestnut. The hope is that that final fraction will provide immunity.

Much of the support for the research farm comes from donations. "There are a lot of real chestnut fanatics around," he said. "I'm one of them."

Later we drove up into Jefferson National Forest to see some young chestnuts struggling to survive the blight in the wild. Our drive took us through Christmas tree farms, their rows orderly and neat, like primitive paintings, and past old split-rail fences made of chestnut, some of them 50 years old.

On a ridge of Iron Mountain, Dr. Hebard called my attention to young chestnuts. "This one, from the looks of it, is probably 20 years old. And here. A little fellow like this can be 10 years old. It's small because of the shade. This is the lethal canker here." Part of the trunk was covered with an orange smear. "This slope would have been almost pure chestnut before the blight," he said. Some of the bigger trees had clusters of catkins on the tips of their branches. "They're all fruiting because they're about to die."

The appeal of the national forests is subtle and the pleasures simple: hiking, picnicking, fishing, camping. I went riding one day, up into the Pisgah National Forest near Barnardsville, North Carolina, with Shannon Ledford. She's a wrangler at the Misty Mountain Riding Center. The sounds were muted: the clatter of hooves on the rocky trail, the blowing of the horses, the murmur of bird song and cricket chirp, the squeak of saddle leather. Shannon's dogs skittered in and out of the horses' feet.

Though young, Shannon was knowledgeable about the trees and other plants. "That's sweet birch. The way to tell it, you peel the bark off, and if it smells like wintergreen, you got it. This is a locust. It's the best kindling in the world." Our destination was Indian Camp Rock, a large overhang used for centuries as a campsite by anyone who happened along. Smoke from campfires stained the ceiling. "Mighty peaceful spot," said Shannon. "We used to come here and camp, me and my daddy." Shannon grew up hunting and fishing with her father, had hunted bear since she was 14. She kills snakes by grabbing their tails and snapping their necks.

A robin sang. "Some of the robins up here can make about eight different sounds." Catbirds. Cardinals. Boulders churned a frothy current in Staire Creek as we descended alongside it. Shannon could detect the spots where bears had clambered down a steep, grassy bank. She looked for ginseng but couldn't find any. She showed me other wild plants: Solomon's seal, jewelweed, Indian paintbrush. Her family has a long tradition of healing with herbs from the forest. "My great-grandmother used to treat people, sometimes free, and that was treat 'em till they was cured," she said.

Of the Great Valley that parallels the Blue Ridge, Donald

Culross Peattie wrote, "This is the negative of the Appalachians proper, earth trough to their cresting earth waves." In the valley, the rivers turn placid and broad; the forests give way to farms and orchards and wineries; the twisting mountain roads become broader and straighter—become, in fact, highways; the winds die down and the temperatures rise; and when you pause to admire the scenery, you're looking up from a wayside, not down from an overlook.

If Interstate 81 is a bullet train speeding you down the length of the Great Valley, old Route 11 is Main Street. It began life centuries ago as a path the Indians trod, then served the settlers as the Valley Turnpike and the Great Valley Road, and boomed with the automobile. I enjoy driving on it, and choose it over I-81 when I can.

Start in Strasburg, say, and head south. You're on a two-lane blacktop with a middle lane for turning left and right. There are antiques for sale in every little town and historical markers, one for the Battle of Cedar Creek. South of Strasburg you're on the Lee-Jackson Highway, and cows graze in grassy pastures. There are steeples, and washing on the line. Half a mile to the right, traffic is visible on I-81, hurrying along. In New Market you pass the Blue Ridge Motor Lodge, and in the countryside, weeping willows and stone walls, neatly tended cemeteries and old iron bridges. The ivy-covered buildings of James Madison University are in Harrisonburg; a few summer students are out, in shorts and T-shirts.

At each end of Rockingham County there stands a roadside sculpture of a large tom turkey, a nod to an important local industry. I passed Kathy's Scuba, Learn to Dive; the Star Gables Motel, abandoned; Nationwide Truckers Permit Service; a tiny house with an enormous dish antenna; a sign: Lacy Springs 5 miles; another sign, faded, for the Blue Parrot Grill. There are boulders and farms, gardens and trees, mailboxes, scruffy bushes, white houses, barns that needed painting 20 years ago. Flowers bloom in front yards, and little nameless creeks flow under the road in culverts. Woodchucks, fat and slow, are at the roadsides. You honk, but they don't even flinch. Fairfield boasts a Blue Ridge Moose Lodge.

In downtown Staunton there's the Hotel Stonewall Jackson and the Stock Exchange Deli. In Lexington you pass a stadium and the stone walls of VMI and the big brick buildings of Washington and Lee University. Route 11 weaves back and forth across I-81 and in at least one place, south of Lexington, plops you onto it, willy-nilly. In Roanoke, you'll get lost trying to follow Route 11, but you can pick it up again south of town. A sign at a church proclaims, "We pay the wages of sin with the coin of sorrow." If it's Sunday, you'll notice that the Presbyterian men on their way to church wear jackets, but the Baptists don't.

South of Wytheville there's a sign for Rural Retreat, population 1,083, which tempts you for a visit. The wind is howling, and wooden lawn ducks, whose wings are propellers, look as if they're about to achieve lift-off. A big signs reads, "Welcome to Rural Retreat." Some of the streets were torn up; they're putting in town water. You pass Harpo's Hardware and a Lutheran church with a bright red door. Autumn leaves come down in sudden flurries, like flocks of sparrows. On the back of the Rural Retreat sign you read, as you leave town, "You all hurry back."

*Fringes of stone festoon ceiling
and columns deep in Virginia's
Endless Caverns. The numerous
caves in the region formed more
recently than the mountains,
perhaps 230 million years ago.
Seeping groundwater mixed
with carbon dioxide to produce
carbonic acid, which gradually
opened passageways in
limestone laid down by an
ancient sea. Further water
seepage dissolved and deposited
calcite, creating weird
formations. Gary Berdeaux,
owner of the caves near New
Market, examines a translucent,
multicolored ribbon of calcite
aptly called "bacon."*

*In a jumble of ravines and ridges, the Blue Ridge meets the Great Smokies.
Autumn paints red maples (left), one of the most widespread tree species in
the eastern forests. Some botanists credit the general north-south
alignment of the Appalachians in part for the rich plant diversity: No
mountain barrier blocked the southern drift of species during the Ice Age.*

*PRECEDING PAGES: Sunset and peace lure an angler to the upper New
River. "While you fish," writes one Blue Ridge fisherman, "the contours
of familiar horizons come to structure and shelter one's thoughts."*

STEPHEN J. SHALUTA, JR.

A glass-smooth Shenandoah River mirrors a bright October evening just above its confluence with the Potomac at Harpers Ferry, West Virginia. The river's two branches meander across the Shenandoah Valley before joining to form this main stem. Morning breezes raise a glittering ripple on the water where two fishermen angle for smallmouth bass or catfish. A great blue heron, common in the region, awaits a meal of fish.

CARL E. MOSER (UPPER AND LOWER)

Fairyland of ice and snow glistens in the Nantahala National Forest (left). On the summit of White Top Mountain in Virginia (top), late winter's fog and cloud freeze into granular rime ice, transforming trees into mysterious, contorted forms. Roan Mountain (above) offers a clear view of Mount Mitchell, at 6,684 feet the highest peak in the East.

FOLLOWING PAGES: Howard's Creek meanders near snow-dusted Elk Knob in North Carolina. In winter "the mountains' bones poke through," writes Annie Dillard, "all shoulder and knob and shin."

WILLIAM A. BAKE

THE PARKS

The Blue Ridge Parkway, winding along mountain crests, overlooks the habitat of hundreds of black bears. It connects Shenandoah National Park with Great Smoky Mountains National Park.

WITHIN THE WINDING 500-MILE LENGTH of the Blue Ridge Range, there twist and turn three rustic and woodsy highways, all connected, whose entire length can be driven without leaving land administered by the National Park Service. At either end of this thoroughfare, national parks enfold the road like green cocoons.

In the north, Shenandoah National Park is threaded by Skyline Drive, which runs for 105 miles between Front Royal and Waynesboro, Virginia. At Waynesboro, the Blue Ridge Parkway takes over, stretching south for another 470 miles to the border of Great Smoky Mountains National Park in North Carolina. There it connects with a scenic highway that meanders for 30 miles across the Smokies. All together they comprise a well-kept, limited-access preserve, in many ways the longest national park area in the U. S.

Early in the 20th century, residents of the Shenandoah Valley began looking to the mountains for recreation and for parkland, even though much of the northern Blue Ridge had been overlogged and overfarmed. Bare hillsides channeled muddy runoff into streams, and the rich and diverse wildlife that had once supported settlers was seriously overhunted and overfished. Soils thin to begin with had been exhausted of their nutrients.

At the same time, leaders of the Commonwealth of Virginia were beginning to see tourism as an economic plus. And in the early 1920s the National Park Service noted a need for a national park in the southern Appalachians.

In 1926, Congress authorized a national park in Virginia's Blue Ridge. Because federal money had never before been used to buy parkland, President Calvin Coolidge ruled that the land be donated by the Commonwealth of Virginia. A blanket condemnation act was passed by Virginia that forced owners to sell homes and lands. Many owners had tenants in what was to become the park. Old agreements between these people—who could stay, for how long, and under what conditions—changed as the land changed owners. While there were some willing sellers, most owners were not happy, and a few took the issue through the courts, which upheld the condemnation act. A few residents were given permission to stay on the land for the rest of their lives. Nearly 280 square miles were secured and donated by Virginia to the federal government. In all, 465 families had to leave.

Visitors to the park hike over 500 miles of trails—including 95 miles of the Appalachian Trail—picnic, fish, admire autumn leaves, or just drive through, stopping at scenic overlooks to peer off into the blue haze. Skyline Drive was begun in 1931 as a combined state and federal drought-relief project.

About 200 kinds of birds can be seen in the park. Black bears and deer are now plentiful, in habitat that did not exist when the park was established. The denuded hillsides have recovered, filling first with shrubs, then locust and pine, and finally with the oak and hickory that constitute a mature deciduous forest. About 95 percent of the park is now forested, with a hundred or so kinds of trees. Shenandoah is renowned for its population of 12 or more species of salamanders. Of poisonous snakes there are two, the timber rattlesnake and the copperhead.

Native-stone bridges along the Blue Ridge Parkway show the skill of immigrant Spanish and Italian stonemasons. Local men and members of the Depression-era Civilian Conservation Corps worked on construction of the bridges and the parkway.

Herbert Hoover, both during and after his Presidency, enjoyed visiting a "camp" in Shenandoah Park where he enthusiastically fished for trout. He wrote a small book about his hobby: *Fishing for Fun and to Wash Your Soul*. He noted, "Fishing reduces the ego in Presidents and former Presidents, for at fishing most men are not equal to boys." He also quoted Izaak Walton: "We may say of angling, as Dr. Boteler said of strawberries: 'Doubtless God could have made a better berry, but doubtless God never did.'" Hoover's camp exists still, presently in the midst of a major renovation.

The Shenandoah is a park of restful pleasures, and more than two million people come each year to enjoy them.

But what of those 465 families removed from the park? Some left happily. Most left unwillingly, however, and a few were forcibly removed. What became of them, and how do their families feel about what happened to them?

I heard part of the story, and got an earful as well, in Madison County, Virginia. Madison is a largely rural and rather poor county that abuts the park on the east about halfway down its length. Total population of the county barely exceeds 12,000, and the average per capita income in 1994 was $16,090.

"Our people were taken advantage of in the creation of that park," Bill Gimbel told me. "Lied to. Cheated. We're still emotional about it." Bill is a land surveyor in Madison County, and I sat with him in his office, along with Leri Thomas and James Jarrell, all then members of the Madison County Preservation Coalition, an angry group keeping an eye on Shenandoah. "People weren't paid a fair price," Bill said, " and they were told that they could hunt and fish on the land, that they could continue to use it just like it was their own. Many were told they could live out their lives in their cabins."

Bill and his friends perhaps are angered most by the commonly accepted depiction of their ancestors: as illiterate, inbred, and disease-ridden squatters living in sin. Historian Alberta Pierson Hannum wrote, "Probably no other group of people in the world have been so much caricatured, with so little actually known about them, as our southern mountain people."

The stereotypical hillbilly is a myth that was never accurate, Bill told me, and showed me a study done by two researchers from the University of Virginia. They studied the Nicholson family, of Nicholson Hollow, as they were from 1732 until the early 20th century, and found that reality did not fit the convention. They constructed a Nicholson genealogy back to 1732; found that, at various periods, all but six of 91 marriages were documented in the courthouse; found that, far from being squatters, of 23 households eight owned farms clear of mortgage, one owned a house, six rented farms, and eight rented houses; found a third of the people literate; found the Nicholsons to be churchgoers and generally healthy.

"My grandparents lived into their 80s," said Bill, "and my great-grandmother lived to 94. They died openly bitter. They died displaced. They died without a heritage and without their dignity. My grandfather missed his home every day of his life after being run off his land. About 15 or 20 years before he died, he hewed out logs to build a replica of his home on ten acres of his grandfather's land that the park hadn't taken. But he was never able to get clear title, so he stored the logs.

"After the doctor told him that he had cancer and had less than six months to live, he built his cabin in his backyard. He insisted on doing it by himself. And then he died."

Leri added, "The mountain culture had integrity, just as the American Indian and the slave cultures had, and it was treated with about the same disregard."

"We were robbed of our innocence," said Bill. "But if they'd just not bother us anymore, we could almost live with it."

A new issue, however, has reopened old wounds. The park boundary, when established, enclosed an area of 160,000 acres. Later, some 30,000 acres were added, most of them federal land. But the so-called authorized boundary that Congress approved encompasses nearly three times that, about 521,000 acres, a perimeter that has never been legally described. A park that large would include lands now occupied by descendants, like Bill, of people who were removed from the park back in the thirties.

At the time of my visit the park was conducting a "related lands study": to examine property within the 521,000 acres and identify resources that deserve protection; to decide which resources are most important; to map them; to help state, local, and private interests decide how to protect those resources; and to develop information that would help Congress if it ever decided to enlarge the park to its authorized limits.

This frightens some people of Madison County almost to death, and the prospect of investigators from the University of Virginia, under contract with the Park Service, prowling around their county assessing resources makes Bill and his friends fear that history is about to repeat itself. "This is unconscionable," says Bill. "We've had this 'authorized boundary' issue hanging over our heads all these years."

I visited park headquarters in Luray, and there put the question—"Are these families going to be moved *again?*"—to then assistant superintendent Paul Anderson and management assistant Sandy Rives. Almost certainly not, they said.

"Rockingham and Albemarle Counties were writing land-use plans. We asked them if they would like to participate in the related lands study," said Paul. "Both counties' boards of supervisors agreed to because the study would help them determine which of the lands that fall within the 521,000-acre boundary are worth protecting in some way—which are important to the park, which are important to the counties. The study will also identify those lands that are no longer important to protect and could be excluded from the park through legislation."

"I guess we haven't done a very good job of communicating to the people in Madison County what we're doing," said Sandy. "Some of the early meetings were rough, and Madison County has since declined to participate further in the study.

"We're not trying to say that the early removal never happened. We've said that if we had to do it again, we'd do it another way. Numerous techniques have been established by the Park Service for acquiring land. There are leasebacks, for instance, or easements; all sorts of techniques. But each time we meet with the people in Madison County, they take us back to 1935. And we can't undo the past." The study is now on hold due to funding problems.

Another sore point: road access to the park. Though the county abuts the park, and though county roads run right up to the boundary of the park, chains across the roads there bar the way in. If Madison Countians want to get onto Skyline Drive, they must make a 25-mile drive either north or south to an entrance. "President Hoover had agreed that Madison County would have the main road," said Paul, "and Congress passed legislation favoring it, but President Roosevelt vetoed it. He was opposed to splitting the park up into too many pieces. He said the interests of the nation as a whole are greater than the interests of Madison County. But again, it's not FDR who is blamed for the lack of access, it's the Park Service." Regardless, Madison County has not benefited economically from the park, as have other Virginia counties.

E arlier in the summer, I had seen a television report entitled "Clearing the Air in the Blue Ridge Mountains." A narrator, standing on Skyline Drive, intoned for the camera, "On a clear day, 60 years ago, you could see Washington, D.C., from here. But these days the Blue Ridge Mountains are in a blue haze that is increasingly man-made. Environmentalists are pushing the alarm button." The reporter went on to note that polluted air carrying high levels of acids from factories and utility plants is worse here than in any other park in the country, and that it may get even more so: 20 new power plants had filed for permits in Virginia.

"Air pollution is the number one, most critical issue facing the future of Shenandoah National Park," said Paul, when I asked about it. "Visibility from Skyline Drive—which was conceived and built to provide panoramic vistas into the Shenandoah Valley and the Piedmont—is 50 percent less than it was in 1950 because of air pollution. In our monitoring, we didn't record one good day— which we define as one on which we have visibility of 30 miles or more—in July. And I think we had just three good days in August. Because we're sitting directly on the Blue Ridge, we get hit by eastern and southeastern as well as western air."

Despite dirty air and controversies at its border, Shenandoah is an easy park to enjoy. I spent a few days at Skyland, one of the lodges that offer overnight accommodations in the park, and devoted warm days and cool nights to roaming with binoculars and camera, to watching the deer browse in the large open area of Big Meadows, to hobnobbing with the other tourists, to wandering in and out of rangers' nighttime slide shows.

During my walks I kept my eyes open for signs of early settlers. This land was inhabited for 150 years before it became a park, so evidence of the pioneers is plentiful. Periwinkle often marks the sites of former dooryards and old cemeteries, and evergreen ground cover sometimes indicates a vanished homestead. Burdock, a weed that has high nitrogen requirements, frequently grows in aban-

In early morning autumn fog, a pileated woodpecker clings to a dogwood tree. North America's largest woodpecker, except for the possibly extinct ivory-billed, the pileated prefers to live in mature deciduous forests, where it hammers out large oval nesting and roosting cavities, usually in dead trees.

BILL LEA

doned barnyards and pig lots. Clumps of boxwood, lilac, forsythia, snowball bushes, spirea, roses—all can hint at a long-lost home.

From Skyline Drive the profile of Stony Man—the second highest peak in the park—resembles a reclining, bearded man. One morning after breakfast I walked the gentle trail up to the rocks that form his face. The woods were quiet, with just gnats buzzing and birds chirping to break the silence. It was late in the year for wildflowers, but along the trail grew some lavender, daisy-like blooms. A dead chestnut sprawled on the ground, and a mountain ash heavy with red berries nodded nearby.

At the top I sat for a while on the smooth rocks of Stony Man, with a breeze to keep the gnats off and Luray barely visible through the blue-gray haze in the distance. I wondered how much was natural and how much man-made. Hawks played in thermals over the valley. From Skyland came the annoying *beep beep beep* of a truck backing up. A monarch butterfly came whipping by in the wind, seemingly out of control.

Off to my right, and down, the gray ribbon of Skyline Drive meandered southward to its junction with the Blue Ridge Parkway at Rockfish Gap. The parkway has been called a "grand balcony" from which to view the spectacle of the southern Appalachians. Proposed as early as 1908, it was authorized finally in 1933. Construction began in 1935 and was finished in 1987.

Counties in Virginia, North Carolina, and Tennessee had fought hard to have the route pass as much as possible through their land. Communities, smelling spoils, lobbied to get close to the parkway. Two counties in Virginia—Craig and Giles—boasted that it "has been stated by a number of world travelers that this route would afford the most beautiful scenic trail in the eastern part of the United States." Developers remembered one lesson they had learned from Skyline Drive: Along the parkway, residents would be allowed to remain, but scenic easements would protect the beauty of the route. Concessionaires offer food along the way and the Park Service provides overlooks and demonstrations of Blue Ridge crafts and traditions at historic sites.

I often seemed to find myself in thick fog or rain when I ventured onto the parkway, but in many ways bad weather can make the highway even more beautiful. It reduces traffic until you have the road nearly to yourself and slows your speed to below the posted 45 miles an hour. As I headed south one day from Rockfish Gap, the fog was so thick I could see barely 20 feet and crept along. Crows—ghostly and lumbering—lurched into the air from the roadside as I passed, and dogwoods blooming along the shoulder flashed white. I came up behind a pickup that was hauling a spinning wheel in its back; surely there are few highways in the world where you would see such a sight. Later, three wild turkeys scurried across the road and disappeared into the underbrush.

Another day I stopped at Groundhog Mountain in Virginia, at a Park Service display of the different types of pioneer fences, and the cold fog was so thick I could hardly see across the parking lot. A spectral family bundled in slickers and scarves, picnicking at a table a few yards away, alternately appeared, then vanished in clouds of fog. Rail fences, made of chestnut logs, trailed off into the murk: the snake rail, the buck rail, the post-and-rail.

One sunny autumn day at an overlook on the parkway, I came across two men from the Hawk Migration Association of North America, tallying migrating birds of prey. They had seen 16 hawks of 6 different species so far that day. I hoisted my binoculars and peered at the horizon, as they were doing. "I got a bird," said one, and helped me to track the slow, gliding progress of a sharp-shinned hawk high overhead.

A few miles south, Grandfather Mountain, at 5,964 feet, looms over the parkway. Construction of the graceful viaduct that skirts it was delayed by a dispute between the Park Service and Hugh Morton, longtime pillar of the North Carolina establishment and owner of Grandfather Mountain. His tourist attractions there— a small zoo, a nature museum, a breezy, swaying, swinging bridge at the very top of the mountain—would have been badly impacted if the Park Service had got its way and built the parkway at the elevation it wanted; Hugh argued that the road should stay down lower, away from his mountaintop. The standoff lasted until 1968.

"We fought it for 12 years," Hugh (Continued on page 102)

A tree-cloaked ridge, not blue but tinged by autumn color, lies along the Blue Ridge Parkway. Forests of the Blue Ridge shelter some 50 mammal species, among them the elusive gray fox and the familiar white-tailed deer. With the arrival of settlers, deer began to lose their habitat—and their lives to hunters' rifles. By the early 1900s they were almost exterminated. Now protected, their habitat has returned. While the gray fox prefers to live in the woods, deer frequent both forest and forest edges.

PRECEDING PAGES: Along the parkway, a pitch pine overlooks the eastward-sloping, rolling foothills of the Piedmont Plateau.

CARR CLIFTON

BILL LEA

Sparkling pools and cascades in the always cold streams of Great Smoky Mountains National Park lure swimmers, scuba divers, and those who crave a wet and wild trip via inner tube.

FOLLOWING PAGES: Deer grazing in a Cades Cove meadow set a scene reminiscent of days past. Beginning in 1819, settlers cleared the high, broad, fertile valley to make homes and farmland. Today's visitors to Great Smoky Mountains National Park combine visits to Cades Cove's restored cabins, churches, and mills with quiet rides and serene strolls.

"There is too much wood," complained an early English visitor of the dense Appalachian forests. Few would object today. The Blue Ridge alone harbors the largest virgin forest stands in the eastern U. S. The tulip tree—its leaves blanketing the forest floor and its canopy towering over other species— is the tallest hardwood in North America. Its flowers, orange and green in spring, its leaves gold in autumn, and its cones that often cling all winter mark it as a gem of the eastern deciduous forest.

Highland farms border the Blue Ridge Parkway for much of its length, alternating with stretches of wild mountain greenery. Cabbage is an important cash crop, along with corn, beans, and tobacco. During the early years of parkway construction, in the 1930s, the states and property owners along the right-of-way

came to a variety of agreements—and disagreements—about conveying land for the parkway. At least one old-timer held off a construction crew with a double-barreled shotgun. Some were granted lifetime leases on their homes. Today some farmers lease government land for pasture or crops, while others maintain a scenic easement, keeping the land uncultivated. Many families have farmed here for generations.

told me as we toured his domain. "There are mountain people around here now who look at me in awe and say I'm the only person ever to lick the federal government. But I had told them I'd donate every foot of the right-of-way if they'd just stay down at this level, below Blackrock Cliffs. If they'd built it up higher, it would have conquered a mountain that doesn't deserve to be conquered."

The section of parkway around Grandfather Mountain was the last completed. "People say that I delayed the completion of the parkway, but that's not true. The man who delayed the completion of the Blue Ridge Parkway was Mr. Richard M. Nixon. Among other disservices to his country," Hugh said, "he withheld funds for the parkway five of the six years he was in office.

"Ironically, the Park Service has won all kinds of awards for the design and construction of the section here, including the Presidential Award for the finest government structure built in that particular year. Sections of the viaduct are nine feet long, and there are 153 of them. Because of the banks and turns, no two are exactly alike. The engineers had 4/1000 of an inch tolerance to work with in putting the huge concrete things together, and not a single one was rejected. Remarkable."

Hugh has irons in a number of North Carolina fires. In 1961 he got North Carolina's namesake battleship mothballed in the port of Wilmington. He's been involved in the fight to save the Cape Hatteras Lighthouse, and he was instrumental in passage of the state's ridge law—the legislation prohibiting construction of large structures on ridgetops. "I'm more proud of that ridge law than almost anything else," he said.

And he's spreading the word about acid rain. The forests on his mountain are being damaged, he thinks, by acid precipitation. Indeed, scientists have found that acid rain can damage trees either by directly removing nutrients from their leaves or by increasing the acidity of the soil. Both weaken the trees and make them easier targets for insects and disease. And if you combine acid rain with ground-level ozone—a pollutant formed by the action of sunlight on auto exhausts and the fumes from the burning of coal and oil—acid rain also slows the growth rate of trees.

Hugh and I drove to the top of Grandfather Mountain, with Hugh pausing here and there to show me trees in trouble. "Every survey we've ever run on why people come to see us at Grandfather Mountain," he said, "indicates that the number one reason is the scenery. If that's true, it behooves us to protect that scenery." We drove slowly up the winding road. "Scientists tell me that whenever you see a tree that's dying from the top, that's invariably air pollution. See those two spruce. Both those trees are dying from the top. That's air pollution, I'm sure. I don't think any operator of a power plant in Ohio has the right to kill trees on Grandfather Mountain."

On another gray, misty day—Father's Day—I left Cherokee, North Carolina, for a drive north on the parkway. Mountain laurel and flame azaleas are in bloom, and, because of the weather, there's not much traffic. Dads at the overlooks are shepherding their families in and out of cars, posing them in front of signs: "Richland Balsam Overlook, Highest Point on the Parkway Motor Road, elev. 6053." One dad and his family are trying to picnic; dad wears a white T-shirt, red shorts, and a red cap. The tunnels along the parkway are dark and damp, and my dashboard lights glow eerily as I pass through them. Another roadside dad is stopping to put the roof up on his convertible, and an elderly dad is making everybody impatient, poking along at ten miles per hour; at pretty views he comes to a dead stop in the middle of the road while he admires them. Finally he pulls over. Big clumps of flame azaleas look like orange explosions as I come around bends. Another picnic, another dad, this one in a black T-shirt, green shorts, and a green baseball cap. In sudden downpours, taillights ahead of me glow orange, like flame azaleas. I meet a group of young bicyclers, maybe a church or school group, looking like drowned rats; worried adults are standing beside the group van, peering back down the road in the rain, looking for stragglers. Here they come, wet T-shirts clinging, hair plastered, toiling up a hill in a blinding downpour. Thunder and lightning blaze away, and it seems a miracle that the trees themselves are not hammered into the ground by the force of the rain.

Just north of Asheville, on the parkway, the Folk Art Center displays and sells some of the finest work of mountain craftspeople. The center also conducts workshops, and I sat in one day on a session conducted by North Carolina wood-carver Tom Wolfe.

The 17 students, ranging in age from about 11 to about 70, are seated at four tables arranged in a large square. Inside is Tom, big and burly, bearded, with a tattoo on his arm and a black felt hat on his head. The students have before them their knives and gouges as well as the finished figure of a hooded troll, done by Tom for them to use as a model, and their own work-in-progress versions of it. Tom strolls from student to student, examining their carvings, offering advice, and giving direction to the class as a whole. "Anything you see that ought not be there, cut it off," he says.

"When you get into carving a little more, you'll find places you just can't get to. Visualize the kind of knife or gouge that will do the job," he says. One student is a little boy, a preteen, sitting on his foot, biting his tongue. Chips fly as Tom demonstrates. "Make it square, then make it octagonal, then round it off." Tom sips at a can of Pepsi. "Now we're gonna cut the sockets for the eyes." The students groan. "Eyes are *easy*. There's not a reason in the world that an eye'll give you trouble." The students fidget nervously when Tom stops to examine their work. "Am I going too far back for my cheeks?" one asks. At lunchtime, Tom eats a sandwich, autographs books—he has published 15 on wood carving—and greets old friends from the craft fraternity.

Some 80 miles south of Asheville, the parkway drops gradually down out of the hills and bumps into the North Carolina border of Great Smoky Mountains National Park. As early as 1885 a Boston doctor had considered "the advisability of securing under state control a large reservation of the higher range as a park," by which he meant the Smokies. Here, too, people have been moved to make way for the park, though the first—the Cherokee—went long before there was thought of a park. The descendants of the Cherokee who stayed behind are sustained by tourism, extracting a little something from most of the 9 million people who visit the Smokies each year.

When the park was being formed, much of the land was owned by timber and pulpwood companies, but there were also 1,200 privately owned farms and more than 5,000 lots and summer homes. Tennessee and North Carolina contributed a million and a half dollars each and the Rockefeller family five million more for acquisition. Ten years passed before all the land was in hand. Construction in the park, in the midst of the Depression, was given a boost by the arrival of thousands of CCC workers from all over the country. Operating from 22 camps in the Smokies alone, they built most of the 900 miles of trail in the park, as well as half a dozen fire towers and hundreds of miles of fire roads and highways.

Cades Cove is an open-air museum in the heart of the park. Cabins and fences, churches, houses, and a gristmill recreate a hint of what life must have been like for pioneers who lived here, in one of the most beautiful valleys in the East. In 1850 Cades Cove was home to 685 people in 132 households.

The largest settlement in the Smokies was in a cove along the Cataloochee and Little Cataloochee Creeks, well off today's beaten path in the eastern part of the park. Some 200 buildings stood here in a thriving community that lasted almost exactly a hundred years, from the first settlers in 1830 to the coming of the park in the 1930s. "The mountains are timbered, but precipitous," wrote two literary visitors to Cataloochee in 1883, "the narrow, level lands between are fertile; farm houses look upon a rambling road, and a creek noted as a prolific trout stream, runs a devious course through hemlock forests, around romantic cliffs, and between laureled banks."

Those romantic cliffs and laureled banks were lure enough to tempt me up the long, winding, bumpy road one afternoon for a visit to Cataloochee. Except for a party of rafters setting off on the river, I was alone as I made a leisurely drive around the cove, stopping to explore the remaining buildings, which are maintained by the Park Service. Squeaky screen doors let me into rooms with wasps' nests plastered high in their corners and wallpaper peeling from their walls. Upstairs, the air is hot and still. The Palmer Chapel, sitting alone in a green meadow near the Little Cataloochee, has white-painted walls and brown benches, with a plain brown cross at the altar. The upright piano, which I test, doesn't work.

The Palmer House, built around 1860 by Uncle Fate Palmer, is a dogtrot house—two log structures side by side with an open, roofed area in between. At the Caldwell House, I tread a bouncy one-lane footbridge across Ugly Creek to the wood-frame structure. Its lawn is neatly mowed and its trim neatly painted, though no one has lived in it for 25 years.

It would be difficult to imagine a greater contrast than the stillness of Cataloochee and the clamor of Gatlinburg, the city that acts as gateway to the park on its Tennessee side. Twenty years ago I thought Gatlinburg was out of control, but I see now that it was only getting warmed up. The tourist industry has clasped Gatlinburg and its environs to its bosom with a passion that would make the world's most rabid capitalist blush. Miles of roadside tourist attractions—theme parks and water slides, outlet malls and souvenir shops, fast foods of every sort and motels for every taste—lure park visitors.

Elegant in form and function, the yellow lady's slipper graces wooded Blue Ridge slopes and barters pollen for pollination. The flower's odor lures bees into the pouch, where the bee picks up pollen to carry off and deposit in another lady's slipper.

LES SAUCIER

But just inside the boundary from Gatlinburg is the peaceful headquarters of the park, and I stopped by one day to greet some old friends from previous visits. Kim Delozier has been working for several years on eradicating exotic wild pigs from the park. The pigs travel in family groups, competing with native animals for food, uprooting wildflowers and seedlings, destroying trout streams, creating ugly patches of plowed-up land, perhaps even spreading diseases. Kim had laryngitis, so seemed to whisper conspiratorially into my tape recorder. "Coyotes moved into the park in the mid-eighties," he hissed. "A coyote can catch a little pig easy."

Stephen Moore, a fishery biologist, is trying to straighten out the trout situation in the park. "Historically," he told me, "you had brook trout on the East Coast of the U.S., cutthroat trout in the Rockies, and rainbow trout on the West Coast. None evolved with other trout. They'd never met each other. But people—sportsmen or biologists—have moved them around." The range of native brook trout in the Smokies has decreased by about 70 percent since 1900. At first the culprit was thought to be logging, which disrupted streams. But researchers have concluded that the brook trout can't compete with nonnative rainbow trout, which were used for years to stock trout streams in the Smokies. Also, nonnative brown trout are migrating upstream into the park. Steve and his crew have been using a backpack electrofishing unit in suitable streams, stunning and removing the browns and rainbows, which allows the brook trout to recover.

Keith Langdon, natural resources specialist on the park staff, sat with me outside under a dogwood tree and told me about other troubles of the park. "It's a gloomy picture that promises to get worse," he told me. "The park is famous mostly for two things: old-growth forests and diversity in plant and animal life. They're both threatened." The trees—not just of the Smokies, but of all the Blue Ridge—are under attack from acid rain, air pollution, the European mountain ash sawfly, the gypsy moth, the butternut canker, Dutch elm disease, dogwood anthracnose, and the aphid-like balsam woolly adelgid, which attacks fir trees. And exotic species of plants and animals—like the pigs—are replacing the natives.

"Almost all the dead, bleached trees you see in the higher

elevations in the park are Fraser fir," said Keith. "The woolly adelgid is devastating them. And the spruce are dying up on the ridges and have pretty much quit growing for the last 20 years or so. We're sure it's an air-quality problem."

Nearly three-fourths of all the spruce-fir forests in the southeastern United States are located in the Smokies. The balsam woolly adelgid hits firs when they are old enough to start producing roughened bark, which is also about the time they start to make cones. The adelgids arrived from Europe in New England around 1900 and began slowly spreading. They were first found in the Smokies in 1963. Over the last 20 years, more than 95 percent of the mature firs in the park have been killed by the adelgid.

The park is fighting back, trying to preserve the genetic stock of the firs by protecting them on Clingmans Dome, the highest peak in the park, and on the road leading up to it and also along Balsam Mountain road, areas heavily visited by tourists. Each tree must be individually sprayed with an insecticidal soap, and because of the conical shape of a fir, it has to be sprayed from the ground. Spray from an airplane or helicopter runs right off. This is a labor-intensive operation and thus expensive.

I made my way up to Clingmans Dome one midsummer day when I knew the Park Service was spraying fir trees. Along the way, dead trees stood like gray punctuation marks in big green paragraphs of living trees. I was shown around by ranger Kristine Johnson. Along the footpath that leads to the very top, workers in heavy yellow slickers were dragging thick hoses into the woods, and portable tanks of water had pumps chugging alongside them. The air was thick with the smell of soap.

"The solution we're using doesn't have any insecticidal chemicals in it, so it's safe to work with," said Kristine. "It's effective on insects that don't have a shell, those with soft bodies. It's like putting salt on a slug. It permeates their waxy covering and kills them. Beetles and spiders and most other organisms are not affected by it. It works on contact; the adelgids it doesn't hit aren't affected."

We stood in the damp, smelly forest and watched a workman with a hose spraying upward into a fir tree 60 or 70 feet tall, trying to hit the uppermost reaches of the tree. He started with a fine spray down low, then adjusted the nozzle to produce a solid stream as he tried to reach the very top of the tree. A thin, soapy mist filtered down on us.

"The adelgids multiply so quickly," said Kristine. "Each female can produce something like 200 eggs at a time, and they don't have to mate. All the adelgids are female. They reproduce by parthenogenesis, so there's no need for males. They're tiny, only about the size of a pinhead. Their mouthpart goes into the inner bark of a tree and disrupts the flow of nutrients. It has a girdling effect. In Europe, firs and adelgids evolved together, so the trees are able to wall off the affected cells. I hope that over time the trees here will adapt and develop a similar defense."

Just up the hill from the Holiday Inn in Gatlinburg is the Twin Creeks Natural Resources Center where air quality is under study. Jim Renfro, a plant physiologist, and Dave Hacker, a research scientist, explained some of the equipment and techniques they used for analyzing air quality in the Smokies.

"There are three ways poor air quality threatens the park," said Jim. "Acid rain, poor visibility, and ground-level ozone. People who come to the Smokies want to see the scenery, and we know that over the last 40 or 50 years the natural bluish, grayish haze has been replaced by brown and yellow murk, from the sulfates. That's one of the things that confuses the public. Some of these processes take place over a period of decades."

The lab had a mobile monitoring vehicle, called the Ozemobile, that they moved around the park to study air quality in different locations. And in a grassy area at the rear of the lab was the fumigation experiment. We walked back to where large open-topped, clear-plastic fumigation chambers, each housing different kinds of plants of different ages, were making an almighty racket. A black flexible hose the size of a culvert ran into each of the chambers, and fans roared as they pumped air containing various levels of ozone into the chambers. A total of 45 native plant species—ranging from *Acer saccharum*, sugar maple, to an herb named *Verbesina occidentalis*, crown-beard—have undergone a period inside a chamber, and 27 of them have shown symptoms similar to those of plants in the wild that are exposed to high levels of ozone.

"We are in the bull's-eye in terms of nitrate and sulfate loading," said Dave, "because of our elevation and also because our mountains serve almost as a catch basin for the plumes that come across the Midwest and also those that originate in the fast-growing cities of the South. But there's no way we can track one molecule of ozone from one power plant in the Ohio Valley or Charlotte and document its effect on one tree here in the Smokies."

"But it's well for people to remember," Jim added, "that you get the air quality you vote for."

I wandered one day through the park's Pioneer Farmstead, where a typical farm—complete with house, barn, smokehouse, meat house, springhouse—has been recreated. I was thinking about neighbors and neighborliness.

The Pioneer Farmstead is the kind of place you'd like to have had for a neighbor, I think—solid and prosperous. A handsome log house, built by John Davis in 1901, has matched walls: The logs were split and the halves used on opposite sides of the rooms. His sons—then eight and four—collected rocks for the two sturdy chimneys with oxen and a sled. Probably at such a neighbor's farm you'd have been welcome. There'd have been an extra pan of cornbread or some ripe apples to take away with you; some fiddling, of a winter's evening, or a quilt to help stitch; a warm fire, warm faces. Warmth.

Outside, a cat was curled up asleep on a sunny stump, ignoring tourists, and a horse in the barnyard came snorting to the fence to have its ears scratched.

I thought about one of the things that Paul Anderson, back in the Shenandoah, had told me. "Our national parks are an incredible value, not just to the country and to the world but also to the communities around them. They're not just national parks. They're community parks, too. We should treat them like the rather needy but kindly neighbors that they are."

Sunday driving at its best takes a group of Roanoke, Virginia, vintage hot-rodders along the Blue Ridge Parkway to a Peaks of Otter picnic. On most weekends, thousands of people on the parkway or on Skyline Drive in Shenandoah National Park motor leisurely or bicycle from lookout to lookout, stop at historic sites, hike woodsy nature trails, and enjoy outdoor meals. When autumn brings crowds of "leaf lookers," traffic is heavy, but those who seek solitude can usually find it not far from the road.

FOLLOWING PAGES: Sweeping around Grandfather Mountain, the Linn Cove Viaduct on the Blue Ridge Parkway expresses the engineering skill that designed and built it without defacing the mountain. Completed in 1983, this was part of the last portion of the 470-mile parkway.

On Clingmans Dome, the fogbound skeletons of Fraser firs (below) attest to the ravages of the balsam woolly adelgid, an aphid accidentally introduced from Europe. These infected trees are older than the healthy firs opposite. The Park Service has treated the younger trees to protect them.

FOLLOWING PAGES: From heights such as this, early Blue Ridge settlers gazed across the broad Oconaluftee Valley, a view enjoyed today

by travelers in Great Smoky Mountains National Park. Once the valley was part of the vast Cherokee nation. In the 1790s outsiders began moving in. Many were veterans of the Revolutionary War. With their families they followed rough Indian trails, carrying Bibles, seeds, guns, and a few tools and household goods to make farmsteads in the fertile lowland of the "Lufty" region. Soon they were not outsiders but a people at home.

Blue Ridge folks, like tobacco farmer Bill Duckett of North Carolina, live close to the soil and cling to a strong family life and neighborly ways.

THE PEOPLE

WHERE TO START. Where, in all the diversity and complexity of the Blue Ridge Range, do you begin if you want to meet the people of these mountains and join them in their pastimes? They are millions of people, but all somehow of a kind; diverse cultures, but one; a universe of quirks and eccentricities in a society as solid as a planet. Where to start.

Perhaps here, in Salem, Virginia. It's the end of the 5th inning, and the score is tied, 4-4, between the Salem Buccaneers and the Durham Bulls, minor-league farm teams of the Carolina League. "Get your cold beer here!" cries a young man in a sweaty T-shirt. There are free diapers and diaper-changing rooms in both men's and women's restrooms. In the row in front of you are a father and his four children, three boys and a girl. All but Dad have gloves that they smack hopefully as the game proceeds. It's a muggy night here in Salem, just west of Roanoke, with a threat of rain. The announcer plays the tick-tock final-jeopardy theme from *Jeopardy!* during a conference on the mound between the catcher and the pitcher.

You look up from your program. The light has changed. The field is now brighter than the darkness gathering around it, and the grass, the dirt, and the players seem to glow. Pop flies disappear into the darkness above the lights, then reappear. Clouds of bugs swarm at each light. At the 7th inning you have some popcorn—salty—and at the 8th, a Pepsi. When the visiting pitcher gets sent to the showers, Roy Rogers sings "Happy Trails to You" on the PA system. The fans around you are friendly but reserved, excited but orderly, generally young, mostly white, quick to laugh, folksy but by no means bumpkins. Much like the Blue Ridge population at large.

The Bucs finally win, 6-3. There were 19 hits, 2 errors, 2 homers. It begins to sprinkle as the game ends, and a man on a garden tractor circles the infield collecting the bases. The scoreboard blinks out. Beyond it, the familiar purple profile of the Blue Ridge Mountains rises, as soft and rounded as a catcher's mitt.

Or you could start here, in North Carolina. Novelist Thomas Wolfe, who grew up here, wrote, "In the haunting eternity of these mountains, rimmed in their enormous cup, he found sprawled out on its hundred hills and hollows a town." Asheville. Every Saturday night for 29 years, from July through Labor Day, the city and a folk heritage group have sponsored Shindig on the Green—a gathering of musicians and singers and dancers who perform at a downtown plaza. Have a seat here on the grass, with a chili- and cole-slaw-laden hot dog and a bottle of beer from the deli across the street, as the music begins. Each performer is limited to two numbers, so the program moves right along. The Queen Family Band, introduced by the announcer with a reference to their "good Christian harmony," sings "Good Ole Mountain Dew." The Pisgah Pickers perform, and cloggers stomp and whirl. A middle-aged woman with a pure, lovely voice sings, "God sent an angel to me that only my eyes can see." Children and their parents dance on the street before the stage. An angry-looking little terrier, tethered to its owner nearby, smells my hot dog and glares at me, wanting a bite. The Asheville Tornadoes, a senior citizens group, are selling soft drinks to raise money for the Senior Olympics in Raleigh. Around us, as Wolfe wrote, are the

Old Glory billboard flags a show in Clayton, Georgia. The Blue Ridge harbors a deep tradition of handiwork skills developed by Cherokee and early-day settlers.

"soaring and lordly ranges that melted away in purple mist." Nearby is Wolfe's childhood home, a 29-room boardinghouse next door to a high-rise Radisson Hotel. A topcoat of his, hanging in a closet, reminds you that he was 6 feet 4, a tall man.

Or perhaps it's best to start here, in the village of Dillard in northern Georgia. U.S. Route 441 sweeps quickly through Dillard, past a Best Western and several antique stores. Just south of Dillard, in the little town of Mountain City, a roadside sign marks an entrance: Foxfire. Here are the business offices of the popular magazine and books that began publishing in the nearby Rabun Gap High School 32 years ago. Beneath a mountain ash that is slowly shedding flakes of pollen sat a rustic picnic table, and at the table, trying to eat a sandwich and talk at the same time, was Barbara Duncan, wife of John and mother of four-year-old John Harper. Barbara has a doctorate in folklore from the University of Pennsylvania and was working in a teacher outreach program at Foxfire.

"Basically," she said, "folklorists study the expressive products or customs that people learn. In one of my first folklore classes, someone asked for an example of folk life, and the professor said, 'Well, to a Pennsylvania German it would be planting by the signs, or butchering between Christmas and New Year, pickling sauerkraut, and so forth.' It was a revelation to me, because I come from a German family in Pennsylvania, and those were simply facts of life that I'd grown up with.

"The folklore of the Blue Ridge Mountains is rich and is distinct from other parts of the country. Partly that's because of the common heritage of the Scotch-Irish and German people who settled here; partly it results from the influences of the Cherokee; and partly it's because of a very strong feeling of nostalgia people have about the Blue Ridge. It sometimes seems like an older culture than it actually is. The mountains here where we're sitting have only been lived in by white people for about 200 years.

"There's another unique feature of the folklore of the Blue Ridge: the extent to which it has been studied and recorded. Researchers in these mountains have been collecting music and folk remedies and lore since the 1880s, so there's been a sort of cultural intervention for more than a hundred years.

"There's a whole range of lore and tradition that enriches the pastime of quilting, for instance. Like the tradition of giving a quilt to each child in your family when they got married. Like the tradition of having to have 13 quilts in your hope chest before you could get married. Like the tradition of working on quilts with other ladies from your church, and then donating those quilts to someone. There's a whole ethic concerning when you keep quilts and when you give them away.

"You can sometimes hear elderly quilters squabbling. One of them will say, 'Well, I remember my grandmother saying your grandmother was just like you, thought eight stitches to the inch was enough, but *my* grandmother said you've got to have at least ten.' They're disagreeing about a traditional community aesthetic.

"Much mountain folklore is intertwined with the natural world. When the moon is waxing, you plant things that will grow upward; when it's waning, you plant root crops—things like radishes or potatoes. There are beliefs about cutting timber by the phases of the moon. Old-timers said, cut it when the moon is waning. And in fact, old cabins seem more resistant to bugs. Maybe timber cut during a waning moon has less sap in it and so is less prone to rot."

Barbara brushed sandwich crumbs from her lap and we walked through a small museum in one of the Foxfire buildings, past handmade utensils and tools, an old gristmill, a miniature still, a beautiful old wagon. "When you ask them why they made things so pretty, they'll say, 'Well, it works better,' but that's not true. There's an impulse toward beauty in them." We paused before the mill. "A familiar saying came from milling. If the stones in a mill get too close together, the grain will get hot and scorch and turn into a sticky mess, which will ruin the stones. A conscientious miller would be constantly on the alert for the smell of burning, would 'keep his nose to the grindstone.' " At an old rope bed that once belonged to Aunt Arie, perhaps Foxfire's most famous subject, Barbara showed me how to use a small hand crank to tighten the rope that, when snug, served as a mattress. "Hence the expression, 'Sleep tight.' "

"Gardens," she said. "I see gardens as a kind of expression of folk art, of people's aesthetic about what they want to have around their house." So I was interested to walk one day with Barbara through her herb garden, which she uses medicinally. Several cats sprawled in the sun. I admired a complex jungle gym and swing set of John Harper's nearby. Barbara looked at it with distaste, and muttered, "Some adult assembly was required."

When John Harper has an upset stomach, I said, what do you give him. "Peppermint," she said. "I've got a whole bed of it. And this is costmary; it's used to flavor ale. Old-timers called it Bible plant. They'd put a leaf in their Bible and it would scent the whole book. This long thing is called joe-pye weed. I'm told that Joe Pye was an Indian in New England in the 1800s who showed white settlers how to treat a cholera epidemic with this plant. It's *Eupatorium something something*, I think.

"Here's my mint bed. This is blue balsam mint, one of my favorites. And this is ginger, or Scotch, mint. It's not as strong, but it's got pretty foliage." Like all gardeners, Barbara couldn't resist leaning down and caressing each plant as she spoke of it. "This is apple mint, which all the old folks really liked. This particular plant came from John's Aunt Pearl's garden. It has a nice smell." It did indeed.

"More than 50 percent of all medicines in the physicians' pharmacopedia come from plants, and 75 percent of those plants are located here, probably right here in this county. The Cherokee taught much of what they knew about the medicinal use of plants to the early settlers. You still hear stories of people's ancestors being hurt or sick and having the Cherokee come and doctor them."

Shannon Ledford, who had taken me horseback riding in Pisgah National Forest, had mentioned her family's tradition of herbal medicine, so I looked up her grandmother north of Asheville. Shy but eager to share her knowledge, Helen Ball was picking beans when I found her. "They're about to blight on us," she said. "This year it's rained so much." Helen has lived in her valley for 65 years or more and had raised 10 children. How many grandchildren? "Heavens! Don't ask me. I'm at 20 something."

Herbal remedies spilled from Helen in a stream. "Garlic and parsley, they're both good for high blood pressure. Jewelweed's the best. I've used it for almost everything. It'll make things stop itching, like scratchy weeds in summer. I think I about saved one of my children with white-pine needles. He had bronchitis, and I boiled them all day, and in the evening he began to loosen up. Comfrey's a good poultice for swelling. You bruise it up a little. Blackberry briar. We used to dig up the roots and powder it up, for toothache.

"I think that somewhere there's probably something that would cure about everything, if we just knew. Wild ginger. There's two types, but I've never used but one of 'em, for a sick headache. When you get a headache real bad? And you get sick to your stomach? That'll cure that, if you make you a tea out of it. It's heart shaped. For the babies I've used ground ivy. That's a little old flower on the ground. I used to give it to the babies for hives. Sassafras tea. I love sassafras tea. We don't have the red. At least I never found any here. It'll keep you awake if you drink too much of it."

Helen learned about plants from her grandmother, who sold herbs to dealers. "There was two herb houses in Asheville. One was Pennicks, one was Diesers, was their name. They bought all kinds of herbs: witch hazel, wild-lettuce leaves, ginseng, rattleweed, may-apple, queen of the meadow, liverwort leaves, goldenseal. That goldenseal, that's the awfulest stuff I've ever tasted."

I asked Helen if, when her children were growing up and one got sick, she treated the ailment herself or took the child to the doctor. "We didn't go to the doctor too much, because there wasn't but one or two doctors around here. There used to be one at Barnardsville, when I was young, but his appendix ruptured, and he died before they got him to the hospital."

Horace Kephart, in his classic *Our Southern Highlanders*, found that mountain people sometimes take offense at the folksy rendering of their dialect by outsiders. One had told him, "That tale-teller then is jest makin' fun of the mountain people by misspellin' our talk. You educated folks don't spell your own words the way you say them." Which is perfectly true.

Even so, exploring the Blue Ridge I frequently found myself charmed by colorful expressions and inflections and dialect. Grits here can be a two-syllable word: gree-its. A waitress said to me, "You need some more biscuits, honey, or are ya doin' fine?"

Another waitress apologized for keeping me waiting. "Sorry we're so busy. It's the week of the Jim show."

"The Jim show?"

"You know. Jims. Thangs like rocks."

One day in North Carolina, in a maze of country byways, I stopped at a roadside store and said to an old-timer, "I'm lost."

"You cain't be lost," he said.

"I'm looking for Foscoe."

He thought for a minute. "Boy, you *are* lost."

Another old-timer warned me to be on the lookout for the deadly rattle-headed copper moccasin.

Folklorist Cratis Williams recorded "magnificent" prepositional clusters in mountaineer speech. He told of one woman who, angered at her little son who was hiding under the table, leaned down and said to him, "You come on up out from back down in under there . . . ."

Baptist churches often use the language imaginatively, bestowing on themselves lovely names: Chopped Oak Baptist Church, Bettys Creek Baptist Church, Gladly Branch Baptist Church, Glory Land Baptist Church, Solid Rock Baptist Church. But when I came across the Mount Vernon Fire Baptize Pentecostal Holiness Church, I knew I was among people who meant business.

Memory artist Linda Anderson, from near Cleveland, Georgia, attended that church when she was little and has painted her remembrances of it. In the painting she showed me, her father Hugh is playing a guitar, the preacher is at the altar, waving his arms, Linda's mother is on her knees, and Sister Rosella Reece, her shoes off and her hair flying, is dancing across the pews. Linda herself is sitting quietly in a pew near the center of the church. "It was scary," she remembers. In the picture, she has red braids. "I didn't have red hair, but I always liked red hair, and I figure if you're a painter, you can have any color hair you want."

The byways of the Blue Ridge yield quiet pleasures. Narrow gravel or blacktop roads wind around the lofty hills, follow shaded creeks, plunge down the sides of ravines and climb, tortuously, back up the other sides. Historic sites abound. Washington, Virginia, has a marker at the edge of town proclaiming itself the first of them all. Of the 28 Washingtons in the United States, I read, the "records very conclusively disclose" that this is the first. It was surveyed by George on the 24th of July, 1749. I had a country ham sandwich in the Country Cafe there, and bought a book of Wendell Berry poems at the Cabin Fever Bookstore. In it I read, "My life is only the earth risen up / a little way into the light, among the leaves."

In Rockbridge County, Virginia, one warm summer day I drove for miles alongside a shallow, sparkling river, past farms and churches and quiet, overgrown cemeteries on whose headstones inscriptions slowly faded: "Why do we mourn departing friends / or shake at death's alarms, / 'tis but the voice that Jesus sends / to call them to his arms."

Rockbridge County is fortunate to have a chronicler of its back roads. A former colleague, Shirley Scott, moved to Lexington several years ago and, perceiving a need, produced with a friend named Katherine Tennery a small, handy volume: *Country Roads, Rockbridge County, Virginia: Self-guided Driving Tours.* I imposed on Shirley one day to take me and her guidebook for a drive.

"Well-built and well-maintained, VA 251 is a major access road to the county's western reaches," she read, as we headed south out of Lexington, launched on Tour No. 13. "It took us six or seven months to do the book," she told me. "We started working on it in winter, and then went back in the spring to redrive the routes. I'm glad we did. There were a lot of things we had mentioned that were now obscured by trees. When we had it pretty well drafted, we advertised in the paper for volunteers to drive the routes, to make sure they could follow the maps and the directions, and we had 60 volunteers. They had a wonderful time. Some were newcomers, some old-timers. They gave us a lot of material."

Virginia 251 did some twisting and turning, carrying us along past farms and through a town and by a country store. "All roads lead to Lexington," said Shirley, "so we can't get lost."

We passed by a prosperous dairy farm—"Usually you can see a heron in the creek"—and quickly through Murat. "Murat consists entirely of the sign bearing its name," read Shirley. "It's said that the postmaster named it for his cat, who was named for Napoleon's general." Occasionally we pulled over to let other traffic past. At Clemmer's Store, Shirley said, *(Continued on page 142)*

Rocking-chair reverie keeps 1936 fresh in the mind of 92-year-old Minyard Conner. That year he and his wife, Lessie (on swing), and hundreds of other families had to leave their homes for the creation of Great Smoky Mountains National Park. The Conners rebuilt near Dillard, Georgia.

Live country music and blues are a free treat for patrons of Foddrell's Food Market in Stuart, Virginia. Turner and son Lynn often rehearse while tending their store. Travelers introduced the guitar to the Blue Ridge. Turner learned strumming and picking from his father and taught Lynn to play. The musical merchants have recorded three fast-selling albums and have twice packed the house at New York's Carnegie Hall.

Mary Jane Queen of Cullowhee, North Carolina, plays a favorite English tune, "The Ballad of William Riley."

FOLLOWING PAGES: A winding arcade of hardwoods shades the glint of trout in the Cullasaja River's clear water near Franklin, North Carolina.

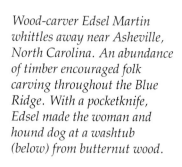

Wood-carver Edsel Martin whittles away near Asheville, North Carolina. An abundance of timber encouraged folk carving throughout the Blue Ridge. With a pocketknife, Edsel made the woman and hound dog at a washtub (below) from butternut wood.

Spinner Martha Owen gathers wool direct from Tulip, an Angora rabbit. From a shed behind her garden (below) she fetches fresh recruits. The rabbits calmly cooperate, content to have their thick fur plucked before it mats.

FOLLOWING PAGES: Memory painter Linda Anderson draws her subjects from visions that depict disappearing ways of life. A valley near her home at Clarkesville, Georgia, inspired this scene.

Happily-ever-after smile says it all. Ray Hicks gets a
big kick out of spinning a yarn. Nationwide acclaim
for his "haint" (scary) tales has spread his talent
from his homeplace on Beech Mountain in North
Carolina—where his wife grows dahlias (left) for
dried flower arrangements—to folk festivals and
record albums. Split wood fuels the stove that heats
the house and dries apples (opposite). In 1983 the
National Endowment for the Humanities proclaimed
Ray a national historic treasure.

Flash of a striped flag warns stock-car drivers to move one lane over for safety at the East Side Speedway in Waynesboro, Virginia. The red Virginia clay racing lanes throw off a ruddy hue characteristic of dirt tracks in the Blue Ridge. At the Westminster Speedway in South Carolina (opposite), a pit crew scans a streak of modified 4-cylinders. The track's promoter recounts how a stock-car driver feels behind the wheel: "Before the race starts, it's a scary thing. 'What am I doing here?' I ask myself. But when the green flag falls, you go into another world. You leave your worries behind. You're in that fast world all by yourself. It's thrilling."

"My son Paul is a balance in my life," says artist William Taylor of Cherokee, North Carolina. *"Whenever I lose myself in painting or riding my 'chopped hog,' Paul pulls me back to reality."* As a recent Cherokee tribal councilman, Bill found himself torn between duty and desire. Coping with unemployment, land disputes, and other problems of the Cherokee left Bill little time or money to devote to his own family. The stress inspired him to paint *"The Hunter."* The canvas tells of a woman who magically appears and leads a starving hunter to plentiful game. In Bill's eyes, the woman of the forest is his wife, Karen Marie, who worked as a nurse so they could feed their family while Bill served his people.

A sturdy chair goes together without glue or nails in the hands of Arval Woody, a fifth-generation chairmaker in Spruce Pine, North Carolina. Woody gives each chair a hand-rubbed oil finish.

Grilled hood houses a 1948 Buick engine that powers the blade of Arval Woody's sawmill. Using a peavey, Woody helps roll a walnut log onto the mill's carriage, which moves the log into the teeth of the whirring saw.

FOLLOWING PAGES: Russell Gillespie of Leicester, North Carolina, turns homegrown gourds into long-legged birds and water dippers for sale.

"A lot of the country stores are closing. The main reason is, they can't get delivery trucks to come out. It's just not worth it." Another reason: the EPA has cracked down on the leaky underground tanks of their gas pumps. New tanks and insurance cost too much.

At the handsome Collierstown Presbyterian Church, Shirley said, "A stop here will reward you handsomely, it says so right here." We drove up to its wind-blown cemetery on the crown of a hill, where we got a fine view of House Mountain. "A couple of years ago, House Mountain was in danger of being developed, but people formed a committee and bought it. Though it's not all paid for yet. Can you imagine vacation homes all over House Mountain?"

Student reporters Tammy Henderson, left, and Julie Dickens interview woodworker Terry Dickerson, 93, for Foxfire *magazine. Produced by a high-school class in Rabun County, Georgia,* Foxfire *began in 1966 to document the fast-disappearing heritage of southern Appalachian life.*

At Lake Robertson—named for TV evangelist Pat's dad, a native of Lexington—we pursued a steep gravel road to the top of North Mountain, elevation 3,400 feet. From its 3,000-foot overlook, according to Shirley's book, "it seems as if all the county is in view."

We took a different route home, past the Oxford Presbyterian Church, where a funeral had attracted dozens of cars, all lined up alongside the road; past a trout farm, "operated by a man who got disgusted with dairy farming"; past a tiny schoolhouse built in 1823 and used until 1928. "They closed it because they ran out of kids. Imagine, not enough kids to support a one-room school."

I spent the Fourth of July in Independence, Virginia, a town barely big enough to support a celebration. I began my day sitting on the grass of the 1908 courthouse waiting for the parade. Someone hands me a little American flag as I note the thermometer on the corner of the bank register 85°. A balloon pops and a child yells. There's talk of Saddam Hussein and his nuclear threat. "Be careful," a man says to his friend, in parting. The friend replies, "Careful ain't no fun." The PA announcer informs us, "We've just got word that the parade will start *almost* on time. Till then, Happy Birthday, America." A minister invokes a blessing: "Bless our little town of Independence." Soon there are flashing lights in the distance, and the parade comes into view. It's led by four Desert Storm troopers, marching, and a World War I veteran, riding in a convertible. The high-school band plays "It's a Grand Old Flag." There are fire trucks from neighboring communities and church floats: "Follow Me, I Will Make You Fishers Of Men," reads the banner on one. MADD and Alf are cheek by jowl. The High Mountain Clogging Team and Miss Grayson Farm Bureau go by. Old cars, Odd Fellows, miniature show horses, then the Independence Fire Department and Rescue Squad in the rear. Gospel music and bingo fill the afternoon, and there's country music at night—the Southern Cross Band—and fireworks over the football field. At "Dixie," everybody stands.

The county seat of Grayson County, Independence is home to only about 800 of the county's 16,000 people. The expense of putting on such a celebration can be formidable to such a small community. I talked later with Robby Wingate, local State Farm insurance agent, who headed the committee of fire department and rescue squad volunteers who organized the event.

"This is the first time we've held our July Fourth celebration in a number of years," he told me. "It had sort of gone by the wayside for the last few years. But I grew up here in Independence, and it was always the highlight of the year, just a tremendous day. So we're trying to make it an annual celebration again. Independence has kind of fallen on hard times. I can remember my father talking about growing up here. Independence was where everybody came, from all over the county. There was a movie theater, four or five restaurants, two or three bars, a bus station. Route 21 used to be the main road south, but now Interstate 77 takes most of the traffic. We're holding our own, though our population is getting older and we've shrunk some in the last ten years or so."

Most little towns in the Blue Ridge are equal parts charm and despair—charm for the friendliness of the residents and the beauty of their old buildings, despair for the boarded up windows on Main Street and the abandoned gas stations with weeds cracking their driveways. Like Independence, Floyd—60-odd miles northeast—seems to be holding its own. The Blue Ridge Restaurant there offered cherry cobbler so sweet it made my teeth ache. The statue of the Confederate soldier in front of the courthouse rises above an inscription that reads, "Stoop, Angels, hither from the sky; / There is no holier spot of ground / Than where defeated valor lies, / By mourning beauty crowned."

Homecoming was September 27 against the Fort Chiswell Pioneers, and I was in the stands for it. Floyd's team is the Buffaloes—called the Buffs—and the school song goes:

Like the tow'ring mountains round her
Pointing to the sky,
Emblem of a noble vision,
Floyd County High!

At halftime the band forms two lines for the King and Queen and their escorts. And as the game ends, 7-6 in favor of the Buffs, it plays the theme from *Bonanza*.

No band played at the Westminster Speedway in Westminster, South Carolina, when I was there, and you couldn't have heard it if it had. Stock-car races are noisy.

I arrived late in the afternoon at the track just outside of town, with a pasture for a parking lot. The banked dirt track had bleachers on one side and light poles running around it. The infield was crowded with tow trucks and cars and vans pulling trailers with beat-up cars on them. The cars were painted gaudy silver and black, maroon, reds and yellows. Most had several sponsors' names painted on their sides: Larry's Market, Dean's Auto and Wrecker. "Your Name Here," one read. The cars did laps to warm up, then laps to qualify and earn positions for the races. There were half a dozen different classes competing. "Modified 4-cylinders, bring 'em out. Stock 4-cylinders, be ready after this heat," intoned the PA system. The crowd was good ol' boys and their families, smokers, in T-shirts and jeans, with seat cushions and sodas. One family passed around a 12-pack of Twinkies.

When the actual races begin, each with six or so cars in it, the noise is awesome. It's like being inside a tablesaw that is sawing nails, with your ear up against the blade. Cars go screaming around the track, left to right, bumping and shoving. They have no window glass or lights, and their drivers are tightly strapped in. One car has a stuffed Kermit the Frog lashed like Odysseus to the window post on the passenger side, his mouth agape in a silent scream of terror as the cars circle the track. Once in a while there's a pileup, and a small tractor comes scurrying out of the infield, robot-like, to untangle them. No one seems to get hurt. As darkness falls, the cars flash in and out of pools of light. Occasionally one goes over the bank and lands in a cloud of dust.

I looked up one of the owners later in Clayton, Georgia. Troy Hopper—a bashful, grinning 20-year-old in a T-shirt that read, "Real Men Wear Silver and Black"—worked for his father, Dean, of Dean's Auto and Wrecker, and was making stock cars his hobby. His expensive hobby. Thousands of dollars get spent on these cars. In the front seat of Troy's car, taped where the driver could see it, was a small sign: "Go Fast—Turn Left." His driver was Melvin English, a dirt-track veteran. I asked Troy why he didn't drive it himself. "There's too much money involved," he said. "It makes you a cautious driver."

Troy's town, Clayton, has a feature unusual for small southern towns. An art gallery—the Main Street Gallery—sells folk art from southern Appalachia, primitive paintings and sculptures from imaginative, self-taught artists. Bright colors, bizarre forms—folk artists see nature and people in offbeat ways. Much of the art was expensive. "Our business could not survive without the influx of second-home people," Susan Belew, one of the owners, told me. "They have the money."

Only the wealthiest of the Blue Ridge communities can support anything in the arts beyond a town band or a summer-in-the-parks program. Towns with colleges or universities often offer more, drawing on departments of drama and music for concerts and plays, or hosting touring orchestras, singers, or chamber groups.

Lexington, Virginia, home to two colleges—Washington and Lee and VMI—supports a professional theater. The Lime Kiln Theater draws more than 20,000 patrons a year to performances in a theater that is in fact the site of an abandoned lime kiln. Back in 1896, lime, a bonding agent in paper, was produced here for the Columbia Paper Mill. Limestone was loaded into the kilns from the top, so they were down in a large sinkhole. Their mouths are now cavelike entrances and exits for stage business. During the 70 years they were not in use, high rocky walls alongside the kilns grew thick with vines and shrubs, and that tangled vegetation, left in place, gives the theater its woodsy aspect. The Roanoke *News and World Report* called it "one of the most agreeable spots in the Western world."

Don Baker, the artistic director when I visited, was first to pursue the potential for a theater space in the abandoned kiln. "It was very overgrown, very wild, quite a ruin, but it had a magical quality, an enclosed feeling that made it seem like a natural place for a theater. When we first began preparing the site, firming up some of the ruins and turning it into a theater, I had to really work to convince volunteers who wanted to get rid of all the honeysuckle and replace it all with hostas and periwinkle."

Don attended Washington and Lee in the mid-sixties, so was familiar with Lexington. "I came here to learn to be a southern gentleman," he said. Work began on the first Lime Kiln season in 1983. Most years a Shakespearean play is produced, in addition to the locally developed musical pieces that draw on the region's history. "I believe very strongly in local stories for local theater," Don told me.

Performances sprawl all over the site, up along the sides and on a cliff face at the rear of the stage. Performers appear and reappear at several levels.

I attended a couple of Lime Kiln productions, one a *Tempest* that had Ariel swooping like Peter Pan out across the gaping audience. *Ear Rings,* adapted by Don from a novel by Lee Smith, deals with three generations of a colorful mountain clan; *Virgil Powers: Backlife* tells of a young man searching the mountains for his identity; and *Stonewall Country* is the story of Lexington's own Stonewall Jackson, an unlikely subject, it may seem, for a musical.

But the exploits of Stonewall successfully filled all the wild spaces of the Lime Kiln Theater. "Battling Anthems" had "Dixie" and "The Battle Hymn of the Republic" competing. The Battle of Sharpsburg filled the arena with smoke and noise. Troopers sang "Proud Valley Boys"—a marching song—and "Hardtack's All We Eat"—a soldiers' lament. "The One and Only Little Someone" was a love song built around a phrase from one of Stonewall's letters to his wife. And his death, in a dying spotlight, cued a final anthem, "Let Us Cross Over the River and Rest Under the Shade of the Trees."

Most of the songs were written by two of the performers, Robin and Linda Williams, familiar to many from their concert performances around the country and from their frequent appearances on Garrison Keillor's radio shows.

Robin and Linda live a few miles up the road from Lexington, in a large rambling farmhouse near Middlebrook. Linda was in the garden picking zinnias when I arrived, and Robin, in a Powdermilk Biscuit T-shirt, was on the phone. We joined Jake the dog on a shady porch for a talk, mostly about *Stonewall Country.*

Like other couples who have been married more than two decades, the Williamses finish each other's sentences. "We basically started with a huge reading list from Don," Linda said. "He knew he wanted to do a solid historical piece about Jackson, something that would attract tourists off the interstate, and yet something . . ."

". . . something that would be challenging for the audience and also for us," continued Robin. "To take an eccentric character like Stonewall Jackson and make a musical out of him . . ."

". . . not just another piece about Robert E. Lee. People thought we were crazy. We'd send a bunch of songs to Don . . ."

". . . and he'd work them into the script he was writing. The songs were pretty well finished before the book was."

The production's title song speaks of "the blue haze hills of Stonewall Country."

"I grew up near here," said Robin. "My father was a minister at that Presbyterian church you came past."

"We love it here in the valley," said Linda. "That title song is really the closest thing we've written to an anthem to home. It's a great place to come home to, after we've been on the road for a long time. It's so beautiful. The light at certain times of the day, and the shadows, and the sky. . . ."

Blue Ridge music covers quite a range, from the lone fiddler entertaining his family to glitzy productions of big-name country music stars. I stopped by the grounds of the Georgia Mountain Fair one June evening and bought a ticket to the 3,000-seat music shed, where Alan Jackson and Tammy Wynette were to perform. This brand of country music has changed since I last attended a concert. It's now as amplified as rock 'n' roll, and the wall of sound produced by the little bands was painful. Tammy sang all her old hits: "Cryin' In the Rain," "Stand By Your Man." She looked good, though thin, in a black-and-gold sparkly dress and glittery shoes. "Rocky Top, Tennessee" may be the best country song ever written. Fans with cameras filed past the front of the stage in a steady stream. "I used to know every word to every song she ever sang," said the woman beside me.

The town of Floyd, Virginia, puts on a smaller-scale show every Friday night, free of charge. Freeman and Helen Cockram's General Store is the site for their Friday Nite Jamboree. Amateur musicians and singers come to perform, without fee, and friends and neighbors come to listen and to dance. A band of three guitars and a fiddle was performing when I arrived. The old-timer on the fiddle nodded fiercely as he played. "Movin' to the top of the mountain," they sang, and "Faded Love." Two or three couples were dancing. Other groups performed. Freeman announced, "Let's give a hand to all our musicians."

Groups spill out of the store and onto the sidewalk and into the alley and into the feed store next door. The Bolt Brothers, young twins just getting started, are in the feed storage shed out back, playing "Orange Blossom Special." Listeners perch on big sacks of Southern States Maxie Calf and Calf Maker and Calf Developer. A man says to his neighbor, "You're not flat-footin'?"—a kind of shuffling dance—and the neighbor replies, "Too hot."

"It all started a few years ago when me and a friend of mine sort of sat around one Friday night pickin' here in the store, and somebody knocked and wanted to come in and listen," Freeman told me. "The next week the same two people came, and they brought somebody else with them, and then two or three other musicians joined us, and it got to where somebody said, 'Why don't you have it every week?' It suited me fine. The older people started bringing their chairs, started being there every Friday night. In March of 1985 we first called it the Friday Nite Jamboree. It's got on TV and the *Washington Post.* Some of these groups could play anywhere they wanted to and get money for it. But they say they'd rather play here than anywhere.

"The jamboree can only get so big where it's at, but I hesitate to move it. The friendly atmosphere draws people as much as the music, I think. There's not many places left where you get that kind of fellowship. One old lady brought a quilt, wanted to auction it off and give the proceeds to the jamboree. That makes you feel good."

On a later day I sat on the grass down in Georgia and heard

Fresh mountain air makes mouths water for barbecue and fixin's at the Hambidge Center, a Georgia artists' colony. Hambidge cosponsors "Southern Folk Expressions," featuring Appalachian arts and crafts.

another group confirm for me that "Rocky Top, Tennessee" is indeed the all-time best song. The Foxfire Boys had been a part of the Foxfire program at the nearby Rabun Gap School when it began back in the sixties, and have managed to keep themselves together, performing here and there and making a recording now and then.

We had all gathered for barbecued chicken and corn-on-the-cob on the lawn of the Hambidge Center, site of an artists' residency program established by Mary Hambidge in 1934. She had founded a weaving school here, hiring local women and teaching them to weave. The fabrics they produced were sold in her New York shop.

Now, during the six warm months of the year, artists can

move into one of several cottages on the grounds and work in peace and quiet.

Peaceful and quiet it was, the day I toured the grounds with Judy Barber, then executive director. We drove up a narrow and winding road, banked with blooming mountain laurel. "I've never seen it so beautiful," said Judy. "And if you'd been here a month ago, I'd have shown you a hundred thousand trillium blooming on a hillside." Comfortable stone cabins, with electricity but no heat, were scattered around the hillside, each out of sight of the others. "This year we've got 54 artists coming from 17 states and several foreign countries," Judy said. "They stay from two weeks to two months. We gather for dinner in the evenings, maybe show slides one night, have some music the next night. Susan Dworkin, who wrote the book *Desperately Seeking Susan*, was here last year, and Olive Burns worked on *Cold Sassy Tree* here. There's a filmmaker here now and several other visual artists. A couple of writers. A potter."

At the Rock House, where Mary Hambidge had set up the looms that the mountain women worked, we had a sip of cold water from the spring house and met Rabun, the dog. "He wandered in one day," Judy said, "his ribs sticking out. He still buries everything you give him. We say he went through the Depression, and he's not about to take anything for granted."

When Mary Hambidge was still alive and conducting her weaving classes, a professor of landscape architecture at the University of Georgia used to drop off his son here to be looked after while he researched the flora of the area. The son grew up, built one of the cabins on the grounds, and has since achieved nationwide renown. Eliot Wigginton, originator of the Foxfire magazines and books, spent youthful summers in West Virginia and the school terms in Georgia. When he finished college at Cornell, he was hired to teach English at the Rabun Gap-Nacoochee School, a semiprivate high school with some boarding students. Early on, maintaining discipline in the classroom became a problem, so he suggested they publish a literary magazine, as many high schools do. This one was different, however. The first issue, published in March 1967, included a section devoted to the folklore, superstitions, and home remedies of the area. Mountain lore quickly became the focus of subsequent issues, as students interviewed elderly friends and relatives and turned their skills and reminiscences into stories.

The first compilation of articles was published in *The Foxfire Book* in 1972, was reviewed favorably in newspapers and magazines all over the country, and became an immediate best-seller that has since sold more than 2.5 million copies.

In the years since, more volumes have brought the series up through *Foxfire 10;* 8 million are in print. Beyond being wildly successful, beyond the renown they've brought to the community, beyond the pride they've instilled in the boys and girls who produced them, the Foxfire publications represent a priceless archive of the personalities and lore of the southern mountains, a resource the likes of which exists nowhere else.

And Eliot Wigginton, though he's still excited about the local

Foxfire program, is devoting more and more time nowadays to fostering Foxfire teaching methods in other parts of the world and to reforming the American education system with ideas born of Foxfire.

I was interested in his feelings about the mountains. "I knew early on that I wanted to come down here to teach," he told me. "A big part of it was the people. And the region is extraordinarily beautiful. It offers a lot of things I enjoyed here as a kid—hunting arrowheads, camping and fishing. Then too, it was the mid-sixties when I started out, an idealistic time, and a lot of us were trying to figure out how to be of some service, how to make a contribution."

About *Foxfire*, the magazine, "I knew these mountains were rich in old lore and skills. I grew up watching women spin and weave and card. I watched Mrs. Hambidge dye her fibers. I knew people did things in the mountains that they didn't do in the city. And that it was *interesting*. If you're sitting talking to a woman, and she's churning butter, and you're thinking about putting out a school magazine and wondering what should be in it, and the kids hate writing—it's right in front of you. It's hard to miss. It just takes being open to the possibility of doing things a little differently.

"I hope readers of the Foxfire books have learned that people from the mountains don't fit the stereotype of the barefoot hillbilly very comfortably. I hope after reading the books they have some respect for the resilience and the wisdom and the incredible experiences that the mountain people had.

"Some of these kids go off to college having published more than their professors. They've already got something on their résumés that has some respect attached to it. I've had kids tell me," said Wig, "that they'll be talking with their college friends about where they come from, and they'll get put down for it, and they'll take these kids into a bookstore and show them the Foxfire books. They'll say, 'Here's a story I wrote when I was 16,' and 'Here're some photos I took,' and 'Here's an interview I did.' It gives them enormous faith in themselves."

One of Wig's former students, Linda Garland Page, is now herself a teacher in the Clayton Elementary School, and I made my way past tiny water fountains and tiny chairs and desks and tiny students to meet with her in the teachers' lounge at the school. Linda's Foxfire class was the first one, 25 years ago, in 1966. "All my former classmates and I are turning 40 this year," she told me ruefully.

"We worked in little teams. One would work the tape recorder, another ask the questions, another take the photos. At first, our contacts doubted that they knew anything that anybody would be interested in, but when they saw that we were going to print their stories, I think it made them feel important. And they eventually realized that they knew things that needed to be preserved.

"In my own teaching," Linda explained, "I try to help the children realize that they should be proud of their grandparents, the quilters and other craftsmen. And as an art teacher, I can show slides of local arts and crafts, maybe sometimes bring in a grandparent, aunt, or uncle to talk or demonstrate their craft. Like a potter. Kids love watching a pot come up out of a lump of clay."

In the children of the Blue Ridge I could detect no differences from their counterparts in other parts of the country. Their icons and

Once a mighty tree, this chestnut stands dry and splintered, the victim of disease. Foxfire coordinator Barbara Duncan explains the blight to her son, John Harper. At the turn of the 20th century, every fourth tree in America's central Appalachian forests was a chestnut. America's chestnut forests have been all but destroyed by a lethal fungus accidentally imported from Asia in 1904.

jargon change as quickly—one day it's Bart Simpson, the next it's rebellious baby dinosaurs—and their noise and perkiness are the same. I found some children one day wrestling their lambs into a show ring at the New River Valley Fair in Dublin, Virginia. With little children and lambs, it's not always easy to tell who's showing whom. One small girl, leading a pure black sheep, looked like a nursery rhyme. As a little boy struggled to position one of his lamb's feet for the judge, it sounded to me as if the lamb said, "N-o-o-o." A man beside me said to his young son, "Whaddya mean they all look alike?" Teenaged boys in the stands, discussing Miss New River Valley, used some of the same terms the judge used in describing the sheep. A little boy was wearing a T-shirt that read, "Holy Cow!"

"All these boys and girls are winners, in my opinion," said the judge.

At the Hillsboro, Virginia, flea market, which bills itself as the Blue Ridge's largest, the kids are like wild Indians, in and out, underfoot, dashing among the displays and tables. Beach umbrellas shade some of the stands, and campers parked with their awnings open shade others. The flea market sprawls across a gently sloping site not far from Harpers Ferry. It offers for sale acres and acres of "stuff": bugles, Beta tapes, old tools, new socks, tables groaning with little plastic animals, paperback romances, dog-eared and stained, greasy parts of heavy machinery, lawn mowers, toys and dolls still in their boxes, with labels now dusty and faded, T-shirts and racks of remaindered clothing, cassette tapes, caps with witty sayings—"When All Else Fails Lower Your Standards," "Over the Hill," "Bingo Is My Lingo"—threadbare tires, fruits and vegetables, popcorn, barbecue, lemonade, rejected hardware-store stuff, sewing notions, buttons, a few real antiques, the detritus of dime stores, license plates, hideous lamps, ugly carpets, ashtrays in funny shapes, deplorable plastic dishes, coffee tables from the fifties, buckets and bowls, cat beds and key chains, doorknobs and desk lamps. There are even tattoo parlors. Out of one comes a dreadful buzzing.

I enjoyed visiting farmers' markets, too, that displayed for sale the gleaming produce of the Blue Ridge. In the fall, apple trees in the Shenandoah Valley hang heavy with fruit that later appears at farmers' markets. The Roanoke market is in a rejuvenated area of downtown, surrounded by galleries and bookstores and interesting shops and restaurants. Here are enormous tomatoes, nice cucumbers four for a dollar, blackberries, grapes, plums—all manner of produce and flowers.

Asheville's large farmers' market on the outskirts of the city sells locally grown herbs as well as about every other kind of produce. Every time I came near, I bought bags of tomatoes—tomatoes unlike any available in supermarkets—and ate them in my motel rooms, juice running down my arms.

Carl Sandburg had a 200-acre farm just outside Asheville, where his wife raised goats and he wrote poetry. Today, there's a walk up from the parking lot that makes most visitors puff, but a busload of fourth graders from Spartanburg, South Carolina, weren't even breathing hard the day I visited. The house has been kept furnished as it was when the writer died in 1967: blond maple furniture, early hi-fi and TV, old magazines lying around, including a stack of NATIONAL GEOGRAPHICS. Every room had bookshelves; one, I was startled to note, held a copy of Mickey Spillane's potboiler *I, the Jury*. Mrs. Sandburg's brother was photographer Edward Steichen, and his photographs appeared on several walls. Sandburg's green eyeshade was in his downstairs study. A 1951 Ford tractor and a manure spreader were in the barn, parked and ready to go. A plaque on the wall there commemorated a Toggenburg goat named Jennifer who set a world record, producing three gallons of milk in one day. In a photo, she and the Sandburgs all looked pretty pleased with themselves.

Weeks later and miles away, Richard Thornton told me, "This is Carl Sandburg's pasteurizer." We were at the Thorntons' farm near Toms Brook in Virginia. "It was manufactured in 1943. I paid $50 for it. It still makes good cheese." Richard and his wife, Jean, operated Shenandoah Chevre, Inc., which made goat cheeses. "Most of our goats trace their lineage to Sandburg goats." Above the pasteurizer hung a sign: A Hungry Goat Is Not a Happy Goat.

The Thorntons bought the abandoned 60-acre farm in 1987 and moved here from North Carolina—in four trucks carrying personal belongings, more than a hundred goats, and their dairy and cheese-making machinery and a farm tractor and equipment. The house, which had been empty since 1953, turned out to date from around 1770. Richard, experienced in restoration, began to work on it. "When I tore into it, I found post-and-beam construction and log joists, and I said, 'Wait a minute, this house is even older than I thought.' It wasn't even a Victorian house—there were no nails."

During the Civil War, a battle had raged across the front lawn. "Custer himself charged right past here on October 9, 1864." Until the war's end, the house served as a *(Continued on page 170)*

Dugout heroes and bleacher creatures pack Municipal Field, pride of Virginia's Salem Buccaneers. The Carolina League baseball team draws an average of 2,000 fans to home games. Families nationwide are making a discovery about America's favorite pastime: Minor-league ball produces thrills just as big as the majors at a bargain price. The Buccaneers give the home crowd a bonus—a panoramic view of Blue Ridge peaks rising beyond center field.

Help-yourself vegetable stand waits on travelers along Route 3 near Banner Elk, North Carolina. An unattended money jar banks on customer honesty. Nearby, Herbert Hoover Yates plows up potatoes.

FOLLOWING PAGES: Dark stripes of tobacco and alternating bands to be planted in close-growing grains form the fingerprint of strip-cropping. The system helps hold soil and produces healthier crops in the fields that roll below the Blue Ridge of North Carolina's Surrey County.

Dressed-up jars of jams and jellies stand in rows at Nectars of the Wild on old U.S. 441 outside Clayton, Georgia. Bufford and Pauline Carnes (with son Kenneth) have operated the roadside stand since 1948. They hike up into the mountains and pick wild strawberries, crab apples, fox grapes, and many of the other 70 succulent delectables they put up for sale. "We know every wild plant and tree in these parts," Bufford says.

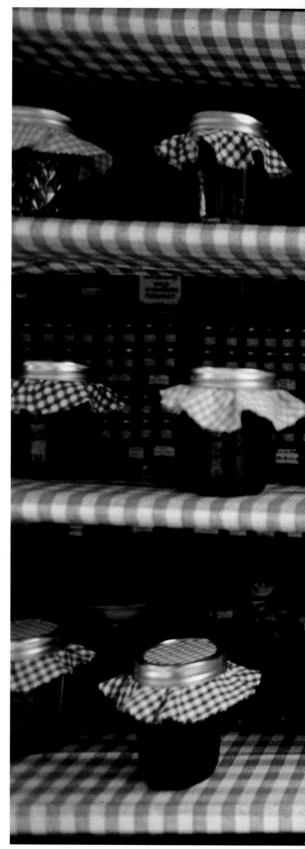

FOLLOWING PAGES: Petticoats flounce as cloggers beat out a snappy tattoo at Shindig on the Green, a summer festival in Asheville, North Carolina. Clogging, a traditional dance in the Blue Ridge, traces its roots to the British Isles and may also echo Native American rhythms.

European elegance at Asheville, North Carolina: The 250-room Biltmore house and the 8,000 groomed acres of the Biltmore estate constitute one of the nation's largest privately owned historic sites. George Vanderbilt, grandson of Cornelius Vanderbilt, styled the 1895 mansion after several French Renaissance châteaus. Biltmore contains 70,000 works of art and furnishings original to the house. The painting on the ceiling of the library (below) came from the Pisani Palace in Venice, Italy.

Autumn ritual: Homecoming Queen Stephanie Huff and her attendants take a turn around the track, while her gridiron warriors, Virginia's Floyd County High School Buffaloes, hang their heads in locker-room gloom. Coach Winfred Beale's pep talk struck a nerve. Down by six points, the Buffs charged back onto the field, shut down the Fort Chiswell Pioneers (opposite) in the second half, and won the game 7-6. For the home fans, the drama reaffirmed their alma mater and their sense of place: "Like the tow'ring mountains round her / Pointing to the sky, / Emblem of a noble vision, / Floyd County High!"

Mountain music makes the rafters ring at Cockram's General Store in Floyd, Virginia. The Friday Nite Jamboree celebrates a Blue Ridge tradition: hardworking folks unwinding to the strings of fiddles, mandolins, banjos, and guitars. Granny's rules ensure decorum, while lively bluegrass and country tunes set visitors' toes tapping.

FOLLOWING PAGES: Thick forests and fertile meadows are part of the scenic bounty of Blue Ridge life in rural Virginia.

A member of the Mount Sinai Assembly of God Church rises from the Cullasaja River near Franklin, North Carolina. Family and friends witness her baptism, performed by the Reverend John Raby (right).

military hospital. Blood stains on the floor are still darkly visible.

We walked out toward a pasture holding dozens of goats. Two bottle-fed orphans, Charlie and Katydid, followed along like puppies. "We're selling quite a bit more cheese in North Carolina now than when we lived there. People think if it's from out of state it must be better."

Of the livelihoods practiced by people of the Blue Ridge, most are little different from those in any other part of the country. The rich valley soil is suitable for the same kinds of farms as elsewhere, and mountain pastures yield harvests of the cereals and grains that are familiar all over the country.

There's perhaps one occupation unique to the area. Horace Kephart traces the origins of mountain moonshining to taxes in Britain and to the popularity of gin in England in the 18th century.

The Scots and Irish at the time were accustomed to drinking distilled spirits, their national drink, much of which they manufactured themselves, from their own barley, in small home stills; Englishmen were content with their ale. But when gin became popular in England, an alarmed Parliament, in an attempt to limit its consumption, passed an excise law of extreme severity, which the people of Scotland and Ireland hated and ignored. So by the time the Scotch-Irish settlers reached the coves and valleys of the Blue Ridge, they were already accustomed to manufacturing their own spirits and to defying attempts to stop them.

The miniature still in the Foxfire museum had been made by the father of Phyllis Ramey, and I talked with her about the past. "My father was interviewed by Foxfire several times about moonshining," she told me. "I'm the only one out of the 11 children who wasn't born in Rabun County. My daddy was avoiding the revenuers at the time and had moved the family to Knoxville. He stayed there over a year. Moonshining was a way of life then.

"I remember him being raided, as they called it, one time. He only had one jar in the house at the time. We didn't have indoor plumbing, and he fussed at us for not thinking quick enough to run drop it down the toilet. I was out petting the horse at the time, and it scared me so bad I was standing there crying, trying to calm myself down. That's all they caught him with, was that. But they tore up beds, I mean they really tore your house up, looking for it. As far as I know, he had to pay some fines, but he never had to build any time—never went to jail.

"He had emphysema, and he got so he couldn't walk in and out to the stills. The men he hired, he taught them to make it the way he'd always made it. Some of it's still being carried on, I think. We have three or four stills a year cut here in Rabun County."

The wineries of the Blue Ridge, being perfectly legal, operate under less dramatic conditions. Thomas Jefferson was first to recognize that parts of Virginia's soil and climate were similar to the great winegrowing regions of Europe, though Jamestown settlers made the first wine in America even earlier, in 1607. Virginia now has more than 40 farm wineries, many down twisting byways on the sunny slopes of the Blue Ridge. Most Virginia wine is sold within the state, though some labels are gaining recognition around the country. Production has doubled since 1985.

During the summer of 1991, the state was experiencing a drought that damaged corn, hay, and soybean crops, but that elated vintners. Conditions were perfect for growing grapes, and growers expected their harvest to reach 2,500 tons, the most ever.

"Want to take a walk?" Emma Randel asked me one day at her 40-acre Shenandoah Vineyards near Edinburg, Virginia. Ruby the dog, named for one of the vineyard's wines, came along as we walked out the back door of Emma's office and up a slight slope, through rows of vines heavy with white grapes. "In the 1800s there were wineries all through here," said Emma, "but Prohibition set us back. The industry really started up again around 1975. We were the fourth in the state to begin making wine. This hillside had been apple orchards. I'm bringing you back here because when you turn around, you're going to have a pretty view."

We turned around and indeed had a pretty view. "Oh my!" I said. Our hillside sloped down, through pasture and cornfield, across a bucolic valley and I-81 to a dramatic bluff rising to a sharp ridge across the way. "That's Massanutten Mountain and the Edinburg Gap," said Emma. "We're west of the Blue Ridge, so our season starts a little later. The eastern mountains are earlier. Grapes do well here, and we're not quite as subject to frost. We're a little higher here on this hill, too, and that helps. There's a vineyard just a mile down the road, right opposite a gap from West Virginia, and it's sometimes ten degrees colder there in wintertime."

Inside the barnlike winery we walked through the winemaking process. The smell of fermenting grapes hung heavy and sweet in the air as we passed large tanks full of grapes becoming wine and barrels of already-wine. Fermentation locks—small glass doodads—protruded from the tops of the barrels, perking as they let fermentation gases escape but stopping air from getting back in.

The next weekend I returned to Shenandoah Vineyards for the annual harvest festival. Several hundred cars were parked in a pasture near the road, and a large crowd was drifting around the grounds, past craftspeople selling their wares, past a wine-tasting tent, past the stage where country music was playing and cloggers were clogging.

A woman's T-shirt read, "Life's Too Short to Drink Bad Wine." Children competed in grape-stomping contests, the toddlers too young to understand and frightened by the squishy, smelly mess they were standing in. Three Civil War reenactors fired an occasional salvo, making everyone jump. A hot-air balloon, in gaudy primary colors, offered tethered rides high over the vineyard.

Unlike wine, tobacco in the Americas was being used by the Indians long before settlers arrived. John Rolfe, husband of Pocahontas, began commercial production at Jamestown in 1612. Today it's still a valuable product, especially in North Carolina, which grows more than 40 percent of the nation's tobacco. Fields green with the tall plants blanket quiet valleys. Late in the summer, each plant bears an orchid-size bloom, creating a field of waving beauty.

In the area north of Asheville, I visited an old tobacco farmer named John Henry Yount, aged 83, sitting on his porch with a shotgun across his lap. "There's been a muskrat gettin' in my corn," he said, explaining the shotgun. "I was gonna see if I could spot him."

John Henry first came to this part of North Carolina with the CCC, building roads during the Great Depression of the thirties. "That was one of the worst times ever. I seen little children fighting over garbage out behind a hotel in Asheville." He's had a number of careers since. Repairing pool tables: "I used to cover five or six pool tables in a day's time. I was fast and I was good." Then a blacksmith. "My daddy was a blacksmith before me. They'd put a shop on a great big sled, 8 feet wide, 16 feet long, and they'd hook a caterpillar to it and drag it to the next place where they was workin'."

I asked John Henry about raising tobacco, and we walked out to the edge of his field. "Now this is pretty good tobacco right here, but it's nothin' to what it would be if we'd a got some rain. There hasn't been a drop here. Not a drop. Last year that tobacco was high-er'n your head. You had to pull it over to top it." To top it means to cut off the blossom, which spurs growth of the leaves. John Henry pulled an aging leaf and crushed it for me to smell. "When it's cured out, it'll smell something like that."

The tobacco hangs in barns for differing times, depending on the weather. "It cures right fast in dry weather like we've had. This is burley tobacco. That means they use this for cigars and smoking tobacco. The auctioneers go yakkety-yak, yakkety-yak. You don't know what they're sayin'. I like to be there just for a few minutes. Then it gets on my nerves."

From the mountains around John Henry's tobacco patch, from the whole chain of the Blue Ridge, in fact, comes a crop as valuable as tobacco and less likely to do harm. The craftspeople of the Blue Ridge produce a cornucopia of crafts and artifacts—and argue, one told me, about whether to be called craftsmen and craftswomen, crafts*people*, handcrafters, hand*i*crafters, artisans, or what—a cornucopia of a richness that rivals the work done anywhere in the world.

Until about 1850, nearly all "goods" came from craftspeople. Things were made to satisfy the needs of farmers and homemakers. But the industrial revolution got under way early in the 19th century and mass production became more and more common. Craftsmanship in the Blue Ridge came close to dying out, but it was revived, starting early in the 20th century, by schools, teachers, social workers and outsiders who recognized the value of the old skills and the beauty of the old products. Mountain people found they could make money with their craftsmanship, as well as gain satisfaction from practicing skills that bound them close to their forebears.

A number of schools, including Berea College in Kentucky, the Pi Beta Phi school in Gatlinburg, Tennessee, and Miss Lucy Morgan's Penland School in North Carolina, led in organizing the Southern Highland Handicraft Guild, which fosters and markets crafts throughout the southern Blue Ridge. It has been hosting guild fairs in Asheville for more than 50 years.

During my travels I made no particular attempt to find the "best" craftspeople in the Blue Ridge, or the oldest or the youngest or the most famous or the first. I went where the wind blew me. If you talk with one craftsperson, I found, you'll have others recommended: "You must see so-and-so." So I wandered the hills, looking up those whose neighborhood I found myself in, or, when I came upon something in a shop that I liked, I'd inquire for the person who made it. I came home with a cross section of craftspeople. I found all of them eager to show off what they do and talk about how they do it.

Peter O'Shaughnessy lives outside Vesuvius, Virginia, and produces, on his forge, in writhing and graceful iron, candlesticks and plant hooks and skewers and fireplace sets. "All you need is a hammer and a fire," he told me. "Back in the seventies, when I started looking for something to do with my life, I tried this, and just liked it. It's an amazing thing: You take a piece of metal, heat it up, and you can bend it. Then, when it cools, it's hard again. Great!"

Across the road from Peter's house is South River. "They call them hundred-year floods, but South River was in this house in 1969 and nearly to it in 1985." Peter, from Massachusetts, has been in the Blue Ridge 20 years. "I sell everything I make, but my goal has always been to be small. Money is not all that important to me. My life is more important than my work."

Peter's workshop illustrated a principle I had formulated during the summer: the messier the workshop, the more beautiful the work that comes out of it. Dark, cobwebby corners, piles of starts and stops and works in progress, the sooty residue of a forge, blackened hammers and files—no hint that from here came the sinuous, willowy forms, perfect circles, and graceful whorls that go into Peter's work. It's shown and sold all over the country.

Wayne Henderson had a similarly grubby workshop in Rugby, Virginia, but there was evidence that some tidying had gone on in anticipation of my visit.

Puff-bang! Jon Moretz test-fires a muzzle-loader. The gunsmith and his father fashion old-time southern mountain rifles in their workshop at Boone, North Carolina. Early pioneers called the piece a "hog" rifle because they used it to hunt the hogs they had let run in the woods to fatten on acorns and chestnuts.

Country music stars wait in line to buy the acoustic guitars that Wayne makes. "I've been building guitars that got numbered since 1964," Wayne told me. "But I built my first one when I was a teenager. There was an old one around the house that I used as a model. I stripped the veneer off an old dresser drawer bottom to use for wood. The only glue I had was some old black rubber stuff of my dad's. Just used a pocketknife as my main tool. Whittled a neck from an old two-by-four. I took some copper wire and hammered it flat and sawed notches in the neck for frets. I didn't know it, but that's the way old guitars were made. When I started getting it lookin' like a guitar, I was so proud. When I was ready to put the strings on it, there came a hot day, and that glue got warm and gave loose and the sides spread out. That thing looked like it had blossomed."

Wayne's father and grandfather were blacksmiths in Rugby, and his mother, at nearly 80, still contributes sewing to the craft co-op in Galax. "My next guitar we numbered number one, and my Mom still has it. The next one, someone come along and bought. I never will forget. I got 40 dollars for it, and I thought I'd gotten rich."

Wayne has since made 120 guitars. "The last one was for a fella in Japan." Some of the wood he uses comes from distant parts of the world: ebony, koa wood from Hawaii, mahogany, rosewood. Some of it is local. "The spruce up on White Top Mountain is among the best in the world."

When I finally found Foscoe, down in North Carolina, there was a craft show going on, sponsored by the Blue Ridge Hearthside Crafts Center. In the big wooden building a couple of dozen crafts-people were demonstrating their skills and their wares. A quilter named Betty Fain told me, "I made my first one when I was 20. It took me six months, and my fingers got so sore I swore I'd never make another one. And I didn't until my daughter got married, and she wanted a quilt. I made one for her, and it was like a disease. I'm addicted to it. I've made probably 40 or 50 since then."

Judy Mofield-Mallow was weaving baskets from the needles of southern longleaf pines. "I go into the woods and pick them up, one at a time. Just the new ones that fall. You don't want any old brittle ones from last year. Soaking them makes them pliable, so you can weave them. This craft has been in my family for five genera-tions. I learned from my grandmother, who learned from her grandmother. It hasn't really changed over the years. Though my grandmother made her baskets to be used, to put things in: bread and nuts and things."

Jane Recktenwald had a huge Angora rabbit named Snowball in her lap; she was gently plucking handfuls of fur from him and feeding it into a spinning wheel. She later weaves the yarn, with silk, into lovely shawls and scarves. Snowball seemed content, his nose twitching, his pink eyes fixed in a distant stare. "He needs grooming," said Jane. "He'll lie here comfortably while I do it. If I don't pull it out, it will mat, like a long-haired cat's." She has half a dozen Angoras that she uses; each can be groomed about once every four to six weeks.

Outside, a young blacksmith named Jon Moretz was working, whistling the "Anvil Chorus" from *Il Trovatore* while he hammered a red-hot piece of iron. Though he was demonstrating blacksmithing, Jon, just 20, thinks of himself mostly as a gunsmith. "When I'm making guns, I whistle the *1812* Overture," he told me.

I looked him up later, at his workshop in Boone, North Carolina, far at the end of a narrow, bumpy road that got narrower and bumpier the farther I went. "This is real close to the end of the world," he told me when I found him. He was wearing a cap with "RP" on its front, the insignia of the Royal Provincials, a group loyal to the British during the Revolution. Jon takes part in Revolutionary War reenacts.

Jon most likes to make muzzle-loaders. He took me out back to where he test-fires his guns, and let me fire one. *Puff-bang,* went the heavy gun. There's a slight delay between the time the powder in the pan goes off and the ignition of the main charge.

"It's not the most reliable ignition system ever devised," Jon said. "Though it's fine assuming it's not raining, it's not too humid, it's not particularly windy, the gun's real clean, and you're not pointing it up in the air.

"The pioneers made their own black powder," he told me. "It's real easy. You find a cave that bats have been in, collect some guano, leach water through it, and that gives you potassium nitrate. Add a little sulfur, a little wood charcoal, mix that up and you've got black powder. And there are natural lead veins all through these mountains. So you've got your lead, you've got your powder, you're in business. It's really amazing when you think about it, to be so self-sufficient in a technology that was fairly advanced."

At Foscoe I also met chairmaker Lyle Wheeler, who told me a joke with a chairmaker as its hero. "A Russian, a Cuban, a lawyer, and a chairmaker were in an airplane. The Russian took a big drink from a bottle of vodka, said, 'In Russia we have more vodka than we know what to do with,' and threw the rest out the window. The Cuban lit a big cigar, took a puff, said, 'In Cuba we have more cigars than we know what to do with,' and threw it out the window. So the chairmaker grabbed the lawyer and threw him out."

Bearded and husky, in faded bib overalls, Lyle was astride a shaving horse, a bench that holds work steady, and using a draw knife to whittle a red-oak rung for one of his chairs. He talked while he worked. "I made a lot of firewood before I made chairs," he laughed. "There's no glue, screws, or nails in my chairs, and they're never touched by sandpaper. I guarantee 'em for life."

Lyle's family—a long line of blacksmiths, cabinetmakers, wheelwrights, toolmakers, and woodwrights—is from Pennsylvania, where he grew up. "I was the first of my generation to go to college," he told me, "and spent 15 years living that down." It took Lyle about five minutes to make a rung that looked perfect to me.

Later I found him in his workshop, a small shed behind his house in Millers Creek, North Carolina. It was unusual in one respect, I thought, for being a chairmaker's: There was no place to sit down. Thunder rumbled outside as I leaned against Lyle's bench while we talked. "From the 1860s to the 1890s was the heyday of chairmaking in the U.S. They'd been built by hand since before the 1400s, but in the 1890s power turning became available, and chairs began to be mass-produced on lathes."

He took me through the process, shaving rungs and posts, drilling holes, hammering them together. Though he checked himself with a ruler, much was done freehand, to amazing tolerances. "The diameter of this hole will be .635 inch and the rung will be .650, so it'll be nice and snug." The posts are slightly green, the rungs very dry, so as the wood cures, the fit gets tighter and tighter. His mallet, handmade, is a beautiful dogwood-root burl, which doesn't mar the oak when he smacks it.

He carefully positioned a post in a vise to drill a hole in it. "It'll take me 23 turns to make this hole an inch deep, so I'm gonna have to count."

"I'll be quiet," I said. The chips flew.

Lyle makes between 100 and 130 chairs a year and sells them by word of mouth or takes orders at shows. "I'm a 20th-century woodwright, I guess," he said.

I stopped by the Folk Art Center on the parkway north of Asheville in early spring for Fiber Day, which is devoted to the use of wool, silk, cotton, and linen and included demonstrations from sheepshearing to spinning, dyeing, weaving, and tatting.

Mary Frances Davidson, an elderly lady from Gatlinburg, was one of the spinners. Feisty and full of life, she's worried about losing her eyesight. "But even the blind can spin. I have these tapes for the blind. If you don't know about tapes for the blind, you should. They're called talking books. I can sit there . . . I don't like television. After I hear *Jeopardy!* and the news, then I'll turn it off. I send for talking books. Last time, I asked for Pearl Buck, and they sent me Paul Gallico. I can't think why.

"Back in the thirties I got my first spinning wheel, but there was nobody to teach me to spin. I went up into Virginia and found a farmer and got some wool and taught myself. Since then, I've taught a lot of people."

I got her to explain to me how the spinning wheel worked. Of the foot pedal that makes it go, I said, "So that's the engine."

"*I'm* the engine," she said.

Nearby, Barbara Miller—wife of Bob, whom I had found making toys at the Cradle of Forestry—had her loom set up and was weaving. "This is a traditional coverlet pattern called 'Whig Rose,' " she told me. "Lots of old coverlets have this pattern, though the name varies regionally." *Handicrafts of the Southern Highlands* by Allen H. Eaton lists 133 coverlet patterns, from "Acres of Diamonds" to "Zion Rose." Barbara tried—as have others—to explain to me how a loom works, but it's something I'm never going to grasp. "I don't understand why you don't get mixed up," I said.

"You do, you do."

Much has remained unchanged in traditional weaving—the principles, the technology. "But the tools I have are better than those the pioneers had," Barbara said. "My grandmother told me, 'Use the best tools available.' She bought an electric churn two years before electricity came into the hollow. She was ready! There's no romance in using poor tools."

J. Scott Begnaud of Gainesville, Georgia, walked into a gallery in Richmond one day and saw something unusual displayed. "It wasn't framed, wasn't matted, and I didn't know if it was fabric or fiber or what." It was handmade paper. That was more than 15 years ago, and he quit his teaching job and has been making paper ever since—heavily textured papers shaped by different molds and combined into imaginative collages or wearable pins and earrings. He uses a microwave oven to dry small pieces.

His workshop, noisy from riffles on Little River just outside the window, took the prize for messiness, but from it came works of delicate beauty. Does he consider himself a craftsman or a folk artist? "I'm kind of on that line between fine art and fine craft. I go to shows and the judge will say, 'You want me to judge you as a craftsman or an artist?' and I say, 'You're the judge.' "

The gourd girls, Priscilla Wilson and Janice Lymburner, operate Gourdcraft Originals in Sautee, Georgia. Former schoolteachers, Priscilla is the artist and Janice the businesswoman. Both are natives of Georgia. They have a small museum and store displaying bizarre and unusual gourds from around the world, as well as the many uses gourds have been put to for thousands of years. They take raw gourds, some of which they grow themselves, and turn them into decorative containers or utensils, birdhouses, colanders, dippers, cat beds, planters, mobiles, puzzles, and gourd toys with wheels. "Gourds are related to pumpkins and cucumbers," said Janice. "But they aren't edible at any stage. They were put on earth simply to be utilitarian."

"There's a long tradition here in the Blue Ridge of using gourds as utilitarian items," said Priscilla, "but using them as an artistic medium is fairly recent."

There's also a long tradition of basketmaking in the Blue Ridge, mostly of white oak. The Cherokee also used river cane. Baskets may be the world's oldest handicraft, though pottery runs a close second. "There is general agreement," writes Allen H. Eaton, "that the American Indian has created the finest baskets in history."

In Cherokee, North Carolina, some of the best examples can be found at the Qualla Arts and Crafts cooperative, a shop run by the Cherokee, where they market their crafts. Shelves overflow with baskets, carvings, drums, dolls, pottery, weavings and reed mats, masks, and jewelry, much of it beautiful and expensive.

The co-op was organized in 1946, and it now grosses more

than $500,000 a year. Of the 300 members, 260 are active and productive artists. "Some we don't see but once a year," said Betty DuPree who had managed the co-op for 20 years. "We buy directly from the artists, and at the end of a year our profits are added up and shared among them. We spend between $35,000 and $40,000 a month buying crafts. We're probably the biggest payroll in the area in the wintertime."

Some 20 years ago, passing through Cherokee, I had bought at the co-op the carving of a bear cub, highly polished, striding along, nose down, that was the work of Amanda Crowe, a Cherokee woman who taught wood carving in the local high school. This time through I inquired after her, and one morning a few days later joined her on the cool and pleasant screened porch of her home on Sunset Farm Road a few miles outside of Cherokee. We talked as her dog Oostie, which means "little" in Cherokee, explored the yard.

Amanda's wood-carving talents were discovered early in her life. "I started carving when I was four," she told me, "and selling my work at seven. I could earn $35 or $40 in a week, which was more than some men were making." A scholarship took her to Chicago, where she did her academic work at De Paul University and studied sculpture at the Art Institute of Chicago, living first with a family of benefactors, then with one of her teachers. She rode buses to and from Chicago. "Indians sat in back with the colored people. Now everybody wants to be an Indian." After graduation, she taught at the institute for a couple of years, then a grant to do foreign study took her to Mexico for a year. Her carvings have found acceptance around the world. President and Mrs. Johnson gave three of her carved bears as official White House gifts to the visiting daughters of King Frederick and Queen Ingrid of Denmark.

After Mexico, Amanda returned to Cherokee and began teaching. That was in 1953, nearly 40 years before my visit, and she's still at it. "It's a pleasure to see all my former students with their . . . I call 'em 'younguns,' that's the way I talk . . . doing their thing." Birds were chirping in the trees outside, and Oostie was wandering farther afield. "I'm 68 now. I resigned about four years ago, but they talked me into coming back. And I'm so glad I did. I'm attached to a whole mess of my students, and I want to see 'em all succeed. That's what keeps me goin'."

Suddenly she lurched to her feet. *"Oostie!* Get out of there!" Oostie was in the garden. "She's weeding. Come up here! Pick some lettuce and onions as you come."

In the local high school, Cherokee Arts and Crafts is an elective course for the students. Amanda teaches every day. "I'm out of here by 7:00 every morning." On days off, she visits her ginseng patch. Her students call her AC. She has seen two generations of them come and go. One former student—Mose Oocumma—passed through her hands in the early sixties. He's a member of the co-op and still sells carvings. And his son Jim became the co-op's youngest member at 17. "That's my boy!" said Amanda. "The thing about Jim, everything's original. This is the third year I've had him. He's begun selling his work. He's as good as many of the adults."

I met him briefly, a shy teenager just home from a weekend at the beach with his friends, a trip paid for with money earned from his carvings. At the co-op I inquired for carvings by him and bought a little bear. It's about four inches tall, a cub walking on its hind legs. It's carved from butternut and is highly polished. It has jaunty ears and a hint of a tail. Jim's initials are on the bottom of its feet—J on one, O on the other. It's holding its left front paw over its left eye, as if it has a headache, or is worrying about something. Or is trying to remember the way to the honey tree.

They stand together on my bookshelf now, Amanda's bear and Jim's, a matched and engaging pair that remind me, whenever I see them, of the Blue Ridge Mountains.

Old ways on the New: Travis Gunter and sheepdog Cody try their luck in the Snake Den, a fishing hole near Independence, Virginia, on America's oldest river. The only stream that traverses the entire Blue Ridge, the New River flows north from North Carolina to West Virginia.

FOLLOWING PAGES: Quilter Mary Cockram of Virginia unfurls her handiwork. Behind her waves an old quilt pattern, the variable star.

Wearing a Stars and Stripes apron sewn by his daughter-in-law, Jack Lombard tests hickory-smoked hams with an ice pick. "If you can push it in and pull it out easy, like slidin' through water, then you know the ham's done," he says. Every Fourth of July for more than 30 years Jack has cooked at Hillbilly Day, sponsored by the Mountain Rest Community Club in South Carolina. Wooden paddles stir steamy caldrons of hillbilly stew. Traditional dress for the men is bib overalls. "They're comfortable," says Jack. "Some people dressin' up hillbilly try to look tacky, but the old-time hillbilly wasn't tacky. He wore what he had."

FOLLOWING PAGES. Belgians test their power in the Draft Horse Pull, a competition at the Blue Ridge Folklife Festival, sponsored annually by the Blue Ridge Institute of Virginia's Ferrum College.

Stubbornly self-sufficient, brother and sister Lonnie and Nettie Graham eke out a living on their farm outside Check, Virginia. They have lived off their land for more than 76 years without electricity or running water. Their grit attests to the hard-fisted will of pioneers bent on homesteading the wild Blue Ridge. Neighbors drop in periodically to check on Lonnie and Nettie.

FOLLOWING PAGES: Gentle snowflakes christen early spring at Virginia's Woolwine United Methodist Church. Throughout the Blue Ridge, rural steeples bear witness to the religious values of these highlanders.

The early morning peace of
a farmer's meadow,
a misty mountain skyline,
the free spirit of a
red-shouldered hawk . . .
these are gifts of the
Blue Ridge Range.

SIMPL GIFTS

S PEAKING OF THE RIVER, historian Julia Davis wrote, "to thousands who have never seen it the Shenandoah is music." She was remembering the beautiful old song:

O Shenandoah, I long to hear you,
Away, we're bound away, 'Cross the wide Missouri.

The song's origins are obscure, and it may have nothing to do with either the river or the valley, but it should. It's a gift from the attic of the Blue Ridge Mountains, lodged in our consciousness like a prettily wrapped present from a favorite grandmother.

The attic is full of treasures. Dusty folklore and sentimental songs, bears and salamanders, dogwoods and flame azaleas and foxfire, limberjacks and muzzle-loaders.

One gift—among the rarest wildflowers in America—was lost, then found again. With the plants André Michaux collected in the Blue Ridge in 1778, it lay unnamed and undescribed among his papers in France for decades. The American botanist Asa Gray found it there in 1839, realized it was an American plant unknown to Americans, and named it after a colleague, Charles W. Short: Shortia, *Shortia galacifolia,* Oconee Bells. Gray and others spent decades looking for it in America. A hundred years after Michaux's discovery, Shortia was found again, elusive but locally abundant, in a dark ravine near Highlands, in the lofty mountains of North Carolina. It's related to galax, has low-growing berries and bell-shaped white flowers, and resembles arctic plants.

I hope the forests of the Blue Ridge where Shortia grows will endure beyond the various dangers they now face. The British poet and critic John Cowper Powys wrote: "We have no reason for denying to the world of plants a certain slow, dim, vague, large, leisurely semi-consciousness." I enjoy walking in the woods of the Blue Ridge. I always feel as if something is welcoming me.

Roderick Peattie wrote, "So these are the southern mountains, 'these be the mountains that comfort me.' Here are the hills, which once loved, call the traveler again and again. The Rockies are dramatic, the Sierras are loved with passion, but the Great Smokies and the Blue Ridge fit into the scheme of life like a good and understanding friend."

Much of the Blue Ridge is public land. The parks—wrenched from the few for the pleasures of the many—gratify millions every year with their hazy rhythms and blue vistas. Though their trees, like aged relatives, are beset by illnesses, their forests and coves still are green magic carpets of lushness, as well as habitat for our most familiar and beloved woodland creatures: Woody Woodpecker, Smokey Bear, Thumper, Bambi.

The people of the Blue Ridge are its greatest gift. Though occasionally dismayed by outsiders moving in and trying to become one with them—"People from Vermont teaching people from Florida to perform English morris dances," as one put it—they retain their sense of humor and their courtesy. They can construct a plural possessive faster than you can think it. "If there's anything in y'alls's book about us, we'd love to see it," one young man told me.

His family owned a track for stock-car racing, another gift of the Blue Ridge. Stock-car racing was born during Prohibition, by madcap drivers "tripping" moonshine along twisting back roads, pursued by Treasury agents. In the twenties, drivers could make enough money on one trip to buy a new Model A Ford. During the forties, according to writer Joseph Earl Dabney, "trippers developed into rip-roaring daredevils who literally tore up the dusty, red clay backroads from the hills of north Georgia" to the cities. Before highway patrols had two-way radios, the winner was the best driver in the fastest car. In 1941 whiskey tripper Lloyd Seay won the National Stock Car Championship in Atlanta one day and was killed the next in a dispute over a load of sugar. His tombstone in the Dawsonville, Georgia, cemetery displays a carving of him in his 1939 Ford coupe.

Ferrum College, a private Methodist school of about 1,100 students founded in 1913 in Ferrum, Virginia, south of Roanoke, is home to the Blue Ridge Institute. Director Roddy Moore has been with the institute for 25 years. "It began about 20 years ago for the preservation and presentation of Blue Ridge lore and culture." A museum on the grounds displays artifacts from the Blue Ridge past, and a model farm recreates a Virginia German farm of 1800.

Freshman students at Ferrum attend an orientation session to acquaint them with the rich heritage of the Blue Ridge Mountains. "Many of these students are from other parts of Virginia but don't realize their grandparents may have lived lives that were closely connected with the mountains. During orientation they can talk with musicians, craftspeople, people cooking traditional mountain foods—local people who have skills that survive and who take the time to share them. Ferrum students also see that this culture has a place in the late 20th century. One of our musicians is a vice president in the trust department of Dominion Bank and also in a bluegrass band. He is great at talking with these students. He's proof that you needn't lose your cultural identity if you go into business."

I asked Roddy if the Blue Ridge would remain a distinct region, if the Blue Ridge Mountains would survive the social pressures coming to bear on them. "People in the Blue Ridge are aware of their heritage," he said, "and they are interested in seeing it preserved. We can't put a glass bubble over the Blue Ridge Mountains, but we can try to make change positive. I think the Blue Ridge and its people will withstand whatever's thrown at 'em."

Doubtless the world will throw some surprises. But a land that was born in the Paleozoic and a people who chose mountains as home take surprises in stride.

"Sky, mountain, forest, and man in these southern mountains make a perfect whole," wrote Roderick Peattie 50 years ago. The same holds true today. The men and women of the Blue Ridge people the mountains appropriately, investing them with joy and strength, with an instinct for tradition and beauty, and with a spirit as old—and as gentle—as the hills.

Shaconage—"place of blue smoke"—was the name the Cherokee gave to the Great Smoky Mountains. The mountains show their great age in the gentled contours that roll eastward from Clingmans Dome, the nation's third highest peak east of the Rockies.

Acknowledgments

The Book Division is grateful for the generous assistance given by National Park Service superintendents and staff and by the people named or quoted in the text. We also wish to thank the following: Zack Allen, Liz Butler, Edna Chekelelee, Jane Todd Cooper, Jan and Nanette Davidson, Al Edwards, Libby Fosso, Andrew Glascow, Gary Gore, Jim and Janet Greiner, Stacy Holbrook, Allen and Barry Huffman, Margaret R. Jones, William and Clarice Lea, Peter Mazzeo, Helen Meadows, Ed Merrell, Catherine Walker Morton, Dennis Overholt, George Reynolds, Art Rowe, Annie Stuart, Tom Underwood, Susan Walker, Anne Warner, Julia Weede, and Jack Wise.

Additional Reading

Readers may wish to consult the *National Geographic Index* for pertinent books and articles, as well as *National Geographic's Guide to the National Parks of the United States*. Relevant periodicals include *Blue Ridge Country* and *Foxfire*. The following books may be of special interest: William A. Bake, *The Blue Ridge; The Travels of William Bartram* (edited by Francis Harper); Christopher Camuto, *A Fly Fisherman's Blue Ridge;* Rita Cantú, *Great Smoky Mountains: The Story Behind the Scenery;* Hugh Crandall, *Shenandoah: The Story Behind the Scenery;* Julia Davis, *The Shenandoah;* Annie Dillard, *Pilgrim at Tinker Creek;* Wilma Dykeman and Jim Stokely, *Highland Homeland: The People of the Great Smokies;* John Ehle, *Trail of Tears: The Rise and Fall of the Cherokee Nation; Foxfire: 25 Years* (edited by Eliot Wigginton and his students) and the other volumes in the *Foxfire* series; William G. Lord, *Blue Ridge Parkway Guide* (revised edition, 1990); Charlton Ogburn, *The Southern Appalachians;* Margaret Rose Rives, *Blue Ridge Parkway: The Story Behind the Scenery;* Carl Alwin Schenck, *The Birth of Forestry in America: Biltmore Forest School 1898-1913;* Thomas J. Schoenbaum, *The New River Controversy;* Connie Toops, *Great Smoky Mountains*.

Index

Boldface indicates illustrations.

Library of Congress ᴄᴵᴾ Data
Fisher, Ron.
Blue Ridge range : the gentle mountains / by Ron Fisher :
photographed by Richard Alexander Cooke III ; prepared by the
Book Division, National Geographic Society.
 p. cm.
 Includes index.
 ISBN 0-87044-865-X
 1. Blue Ridge Mountains. 2. Blue Ridge Mountains--Pictorial
works. I. Cooke, Richard Alexander. II. National Geographic
Society (U.S.). Book Division. III. Title.
 F217.B6F57 1992
 975.5—dc20   92-32429
                                         ᴄᴵᴾ

Composition for this book by the Typographic section of National
Geographic Production Services, Pre-Press Division. Set in Hiroshige
Book. Printed and bound by R. R. Donnelley & Sons, Willard, Ohio.
Color separations by Graphic Art Service, Inc., Nashville, Tenn.;
Lanman Progressive Co., Washington, D. C.; Lincoln Graphics, Inc.,
Cherry Hill, N.J.; and Phototype Color Graphics, Pennsauken, N.J. Dust
jacket printed by Federated Lithographers-Printers, Inc., Providence, R.I.

VISITING THE PARKS

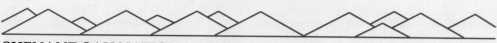

SHENANDOAH NATIONAL PARK

High above its namesake valley, Shenandoah National Park straddles the gentle contours of the Blue Ridge. Hugging the high ridges and running the length of the park, the 105-mile Skyline Drive rewards motorists with glorious vistas. Spring's myriad azaleas, laurels, and wildflowers, and mid-October's blaze of fall foliage bring bumper-to-bumper traffic; visitors are advised then to arrive early in the day and to avoid weekends. Away from the drive, the park's 195,000 acres contain nearly 500 miles of trails, including a 95-mile stretch of the Appalachian Trail. Activities range from gentle strolls on self-guiding nature trails to exhilarating hikes up 3,268-foot Old Rag, from picnics beside Whiteoak Falls to horseback rides through the woods. Winter brings cross-country skiers. Accommodations include lodges such as Big Meadows and Skyland, four campgrounds, and several huts and cabins maintained by the Potomac Appalachian Trail Club. Reservations are recommended. Many facilities close in winter. Snow and ice can also close Skyline Drive.

3655 U.S. Highway 211E ● Luray, VA 22835 ● (540) 999-3500

BLUE RIDGE PARKWAY

The link between two national parks, the Blue Ridge Parkway ribbons the high ridges from the Shenandoah to the Great Smokies, revealing a passing panorama of mountain and valley. The speed limit on the roadway is 45 miles per hour, but 30 miles per hour is a good average to allow for stops at interesting spots that punctuate the 470-mile-long roadway or lie nearby. Visitors enjoy a potpourri of attractions: picnic groves, self-guiding nature trails, and larger preserves of natural beauty like Linville Falls, Mount Mitchell State Park, and Craggy Gardens; cultural relics like the old Brinegar cabin; demonstrations of old-time skills at Mabry Mill; folk art and craft centers. Visitation peaks with the autumn color. Several lodges, restaurants, and nine campgrounds serve travelers. Except for Peaks of Otter, limited services are available in winter. Reservations are recommended for lodges. Campgrounds are first come, first served.

**Blue Ridge Parkway ● 400 BB&T Building
Asheville, North Carolina 28801 ● (704) 298-0398**

GREAT SMOKY MOUNTAINS NATIONAL PARK

Encompassing some of the East's highest peaks, an extraordinary diversity of plant life, and a rich pioneer tradition, Great Smoky Mountains has gained the designations International Biosphere Reserve and World Heritage Site. For a quick overview, Newfound Gap Road traverses the park between the two main visitor centers, Sugarlands and Oconaluftee. To escape the crowds, and perhaps glimpse a deer or a black bear, visitors can follow numerous side roads or sample 900 miles of trails that vary from short interpretive loops to wilderness backpack routes. Half a day's hike brings you to secluded Le Conte Lodge atop 6,593-foot Mount Le Conte. On Cades Cove loop road, you drive past craft demonstrations and historic sites such as the old John Oliver Place, the Cable Mill, and the Primitive Baptist Church. Five stables serve equestrians. Several backcountry shelters serve hikers, and, in addition to Le Conte, ten campgrounds offer accommodations. Reservations are recommended. The park remains open all year, although some facilities and roads close in winter.

**107 Park Headquarters Road
Gatlinburg, Tennessee 37738 ● (423) 436-1200**